The Modern Judge

Power, Responsibility and Society's Expectations

The Modern Judge

Power, Responsibility and Society's Expectations

Sir Mark Hedley

With a Foreword by Sir James Munby

LexisNexis®

Published by LexisNexis

LexisNexis
Regus
Terrace Floor
Castlemead
Lower Castle Street
Bristol BS1 3AG

© RELX (UK) Limited, trading as LexisNexis 2016

British Library Cataloguing-in-Publication Data

A catalogue record for this book is available from the British Library.

ISBN 978 1 78473 279 0

Typeset by Letterpart Limited, Caterham on the Hill, Surrey CR3 5XL

Printed in Great Britain by Hobbs the Printers Limited, Totton, Hampshire SO40 3WX

Foreword by Sir James Munby

Some judges write memoirs, a rather dubious literary genre. Some very senior judges write books on the higher jurisprudence. This book by Sir Mark Hedley is, dare I say it, both more interesting and more important.

It is a truism of family law that there is no such thing as the perfect partner or the perfect parent. Likewise, there is no such person known to the law as the ideal judge. Sir Mark is a modest man – though, truth be told, with little to be modest about – and he would never think, let alone say, this, but he came as close as any first instance judge can to the ideal. When he came to the Family Division of the High Court in 2002 he brought with him vast experience as a Circuit Judge, having sat not merely in criminal, civil and family cases but also as an official referee – experience from which we and everyone who appeared in front of him hugely benefitted. It was his good luck and our great fortune that he arrived in the Family Division at a time when its work was expanding into areas that previous generations of family judges would have thought inconceivable but for which he was ideally suited.

Sir Mark's judgments, indeed, everything he did as a judge, both in the Family Division and the Court of Protection and on the occasions he sat in the civil and criminal divisions of the Court of Appeal, exemplified his wisdom and humanity and reflected, as does this series of lectures, his deep understanding of both the forensic process and the human condition. His impact on the development of the law, particularly in novel and complex areas such as surrogacy, was profoundly significant. He had a remarkable ability to distil legal concepts and fundamentally important principles in spare, non-legal and seemingly simple language. His judgment in *Re L (Care: Threshold Criteria)* [2007] 1 FLR 2050, the key passage in which he sets out in Chapter 4, is a justly celebrated statement of the proper role of the state and one of the most frequently cited passages in the contemporary canon. The reference to 'our fallible humanity' is both striking and so very characteristic of Sir Mark's view of the human condition.

There are many other similarly insightful passages I could cite, but one must suffice. It comes from Sir Mark's judgment in *Re R (Care Proceedings: Causation)* [2011] EWHC 1715 (Fam), [2011] 2 FLR 1384, para [10], and merits quotation in full:

'I have been impressed over the years by the willingness of the best paediatricians and those who practise in the specialities of paediatric medicine to recognise how much we do not know about the growth patterns and what goes wrong in them, particularly in infants. Since they grow at a remarkable speed and cannot themselves give any clue as to what is happening inside them, and since research using control samples is self-evidently impossible in many areas, perhaps we should not be surprised. In my judgment, a conclusion of unknown aetiology in respect of an infant represents neither professional nor forensic failure. It simply recognises that we still have much to learn and it also recognises that it is dangerous and wrong to infer non-accidental injury merely from the absence of any other understood mechanism. Maybe it simply represents a general acknowledgement that we are fearfully and wonderfully made.'

The very apt quotation from Psalm 139 encapsulates a truth as relevant to our modern secular society as to the world in which the words were first sung.

There is much in this fascinating, humane and insightful book from which all of us, judges, lawyers and lay people alike, can learn and benefit. We are much indebted to Sir Mark for sharing with us the matured fruits of his time on the Bench.

James Munby, President of the Family Division
27 October 2016

Preface

I have always had a deep respect for those involved in the family and mental capacity justice systems, whatever their particular role or discipline. As a barrister and judge (who has served at all levels from Assistant Recorder to High Court judge), I have dealt with matters from the everyday to the dramatically unique. I am therefore very aware of the pressures upon both individuals and the system, pressures that have increased over the last few years. It was only on retirement, and the opportunity for reflection that that offers, that I have begun to be able to articulate the basis for that respect. This book, though more specific in its concentration on judicial discretion, was born of that reflection.

This is the product of lifelong conversations with colleagues, court staff, other professionals, neighbours, fellow church members, members of Liverpool Hope University and indeed anyone whose ear I could engage. I have learned from all of them and am grateful to all. Should anyone see an unacknowledged idea of theirs in the text, they may well be right! I am only sorry that I had forgotten its true origin. I am grateful to the President for making time in an impossible schedule to write the Foreword and for what he says. As an innocent abroad in these matters, I have much appreciated the guidance and encouragement from Jordan Publishing's staff. Although she will deeply disapprove of my saying it in public, my chief gratitude must go to my wife Erica who has born with me and my baggage for over 40 years and whose critical encouragement has renewed energy whenever it has flagged.

One final comment on the text. I am aware that, whenever a general noun like judge, parent, child, party or protected person is used, it may represent male or female – usually both. To avoid clumsiness and confusion, I have opted to use a specific pronoun, usually the masculine. I hope that the reader will take this to cover both male and female.

Sir Mark Hedley

October 2016

Contents

Chapter 1

Why this Book?

A distinguished American judge[1] has said: 'Judges, like other refined people in our society, are reticent about talking about sex, but judges are also reticent about talking about judging, especially talking frankly about it, whether to their colleagues or to a larger professional audience.' In so saying, he has highlighted a factor which also applies to judges in England and Wales.

Scholarly works on appellate[2] courts have been written (especially in the USA), as have many judicial memoirs. This is neither of those. The purpose of this book is a frank, rather than scholarly, reflection on judging, focusing in particular on the trial judge.

The trial judge is in a very different position to the appellate judge. It is at the trial that the facts are determined, and it is essentially the trial judge who exercises the powers of discretion which modern society increasingly vests in its judiciary. As society becomes more complex, so does the law. However, the substantive law cannot provide for every circumstance, so its application often involves the exercise of discretion. This

---

[1] US Federal Appeals Judge Richard A. Posner.

[2] Those courts whose primary purpose is to hear appeals from lower courts: in England and Wales, the Court of Appeal and the Supreme Court.

discretion may perhaps be described as those powers that give to a judge the right and duty to choose between two or more lawful and reasonable outcomes so as to achieve a just result in the individual case. Criminal sentencing, child welfare, the protection of those who lack mental capacity, and disputes about medical treatment are obvious examples.

How do judges go about that? How far are we influenced or affected by where we came from, what we believe and our own life experiences? And, if consistency is an aspect of public justice, can that be achieved? What about the conflict between public justice and personal privacy? Many see these as pressing questions in a society where judges have perhaps greater effective power than ever before. As a result, the media have focused a critical attention on the courts as never before. This book invites reflection on these matters: it is a quest for practical insight rather than scholarly analysis.

Thus, I want to discuss frankly being a trial judge, and to describe how I plot my way through some of these issues. My emphasis will be partly on how disputes of fact are resolved, but mostly on how discretion is exercised particularly in those areas mentioned above where a judge does indeed have wide powers. As I have said, this is intended to be a practical reflection rather than a scholarly analysis, and accordingly the book will be fairly light on references and footnotes. The cases used to illustrate points will almost always be those over which I have presided – not least because I understand precisely why I decided them as I did! Most of them will have appeared in formal Law Reports, but the few that have not have been sufficiently edited to ensure the privacy of those involved.

This book is built on a series of five public lectures given during Autumn 2015 under the title 'The Modern Judge: Power, Responsibility and Society's Expectations' at Liverpool Hope University, where I am a Visiting Professor of Law. I have sought to integrate into this my inaugural lecture given there the year before, and then to conclude with some thoughts as to what might lie ahead. I have spent 42 years in the law as barrister and judge, having held part- and full-time judicial office for 30 years; the last 11 of those as a High Court judge until my retirement in 2013. That has provided a fair opportunity for reflection.

What follows, therefore, is a reflection on the modern art of judging. It is necessary to start by setting judging in its social, political and (where necessary) historical context in modern Britain. Even in ancient times, every civilisation has required the law and a legal system to enable social coexistence. The biblical comment (appropriately in the Book of Judges) that 'in those days Israel had no king and every man did what was right in his own eyes'[3] was not a description of Utopia, but of anarchy. That experience of need is essentially unchanged today. Indeed, the more complex the structures of society and the more diverse its experience and values, the more the law and its administration is required.

That leads to a consideration of the role of the modern judge. In many cases of medical treatment and childcare, it is often asked why this is entrusted to judges at all and not, for example, to 'experts'. The answer lies less in the specific expertise of the judge than in the need for society to provide an independent means for the authoritative and binding resolution of disputes between individuals and between the citizen and the state. This independence becomes more important as greater powers are vested in judges. These powers are often not direct but they derive from statute or common law, giving to judges not only the duty (in civil cases) to resolve disputes of fact, but also to decide what ensures fairness, justice and protection of the vulnerable in any individual case.

---

[3]   Judges xxi 25.

A current concern about many of these cases is that they are conducted in private, even though the decisions may have life-changing and lifelong consequences. It is the tension between doing justice in public and protecting the privacy of the vulnerable and those who reasonably expect their private affairs to remain private.

All of these matters are most fully expressed and tested in child welfare cases, issues relating to mental capacity, medical treatment, and criminal sentencing; areas which coincide substantially with my own experience. Although, of course, similar issues arise in many areas of the law, these are the ones that tend to attract most public attention. I plan to consider these issues in a little detail, especially the tension between protection and autonomy which lies at the heart of much controversy in these areas and which, with an ageing population, will not diminish in importance.

While I was a serving judge I became increasingly concerned that many in society are simply unaware of these powers, especially the discretionary powers, vested in the modern judge. One of my purposes is to offer some description and explanation of those powers. In a democratic society, these powers should be exercised by the judges with the consent of that society. If there is no proper understanding of these powers, how can there be proper consent to their use? Moreover, the use of these powers involves society placing extensive trust in judges to exercise them properly. On what basis may such trust be given? Is it a trust that our judges can actually justify or fulfil? These are some of the issues on which I would like to reflect and which I believe to be of some importance in the life of our society, with its inherent sense of fairness and desire for justice.

Chapter 2

Judges Today – What is their Role?

In any discussion about the law in this country, the focus of most people is on criminal law. Yet it is not in this area that the powers of judges have so expanded over the last 40 years that I have been in practice. Although many changes have been made in criminal law and procedure, the essence of the criminal process would be immediately recognised by a 19th-century judge. This expansion of power has been seen primarily in civil law: in housing, in family law, and in the law relating to the mentally ill and those who lack capacity to make their own decisions. The emphasis in this book will be on family and mental capacity law; partly because they have seen a dramatic growth in discretionary power, and partly because my own experience lies primarily in those fields.

Those, indeed, are the two areas where discretion is most controversial, but it is not confined to them. In housing law, for example, a judge may have to decide not only whether a landlord is entitled to a possession order, but also whether in all the circumstances it is 'reasonable' to grant it. That may involve a judge considering a tenant's own personal position, the actual reasons for default, and so on. Interestingly, this is an area where Parliament has intervened to restrict discretion by providing for circumstances in which the court 'must' grant possession. Again, where a court is considering an interim injunction before trial, it will not only consider whether the claimant has a good, arguable case (an essential qualification), but whether, even so, it is 'just and convenient' to grant an injunction. So, where tenants were resisting demolition of their homes on the basis that they had not been adequately consulted by the local authority landlord, the County Court granted an injunction against demolition (even though that meant contractors having to leave properties on which work had already been started) until after the trial of the consultation issue. Clearly, if householders had won but their properties had been demolished, that would have been unjust. Equally, if (as was the case) the local authority were successful, they would have suffered losses for which their tenants could not compensate them. The provision for an interim injunction is designed to enable the judge to achieve the closest to fairness in the individual case.

There are very few prescriptive rules in relation to the exercise of discretion. Judges are entrusted with wide powers to achieve just solutions in individual cases. I want to reflect not only on what those powers are and how they are used, but also on the values and principles on which they are exercised and where such values and principles have come from. These matters, especially in the fields of family and mental incapacity law, lie at the heart of our system, and in the end depend on the informed consent of the society in which those powers are exercised.

The areas under consideration are value-laden and every outcome will have involved a value judgment made by the decision-maker. We are concerned with those decisions made by a judge. For the system to be credible, those value judgments must be credible. If they are not, then the informed consent of society is not there. The difficulty today is in determining what those values are to which society generally (not just particular parts of it) subscribes. That really can sometimes seem like a chasing of the wind.

There is a further reason why this question of discretion is important. The appellate courts have been very reluctant to interfere with discretionary decisions. They will readily intervene if they think that the judge has got the law wrong in any way. They will be prepared cautiously to intervene over questions of fact, particularly where based on documents or inference. They are, however, very reticent if a judge, having the relevant experience and expertise and having got those matters right, exercises discretion and comes to a conclusion which was reasonably open on the evidence. Nowhere is this more so than when issues of 'welfare' or 'best interests' are under consideration in a family or mental capacity case.

There was a very difficult case in which an English woman entered into a surrogacy agreement with an American commissioning couple.[1] She was allowed under the agreement to return home to have the twin babies, but she then refused to return them to the couple in California and remained in this country. The case raised difficult issues of both jurisdiction and welfare. The first were matters of law and the parties accepted the trial judge's conclusions on that. The second, however, were matters of discretion and remained in contention. Permission to appeal was sought on the basis of the unique difficulties of the case. In refusing that permission, the Court of Appeal is said to have remarked that the unique difficulties explained why the case had been assigned to a High Court judge, and they were for that judge to resolve in the exercise of discretion.

Were I to review what I see as my 20 most interesting or demanding cases, no more than two or three will have gone on appeal. That is not to say that I must have been right in the others, but rather that they were exercises of discretion which were in effect beyond challenge or I had achieved a solution with which all parties decided that they could or must live. The

---

[1]   *W & B v H (Child Abduction: Surrogacy)* [2002] 1 FLR 1008, [2002] 2 FLR 252.

difficulty of challenge makes understanding discretion very important and we shall return to it again in our reflections.

It remains true that many judges come from similar cultural stables, though that is changing all the time. The changes are at present much more evident among the younger and more junior judiciary. It remains to be seen the extent to which gender equality in numbers among lawyers under 30, as we presently have, is reflected in due course in judicial appointments at all levels of seniority. Everyone is agreed that the judiciary should reflect the diversity of the society they serve, just as everyone is agreed that judicial appointments should be on merit alone. The difficulty is in working that out in practice, given the wide range of individual opportunity and aspiration. Judges do, however, tend to be very diverse in their own moral, political, and philosophical views. Indeed, there will hardly be a view which can be lawfully expressed in our society which will not be represented somewhere in the judiciary. Moreover, judges tend to have quite strong personal value systems. That will probably be something that inclined them to be a judge in the first place. The value-free judge does not and should not exist.

Judges are, however, united in one view: their own fallibility. None of us is right all the time; no human being ever is. You cannot do the job I did for very long without that becoming very apparent. Humility is an essential quality of the good judge, not always easy to reconcile with the confidence needed to make the decision for which all the parties are waiting.

For us to understand and scrutinise the role of the modern judge, it is necessary to have some historical and philosophical context, for judges have been on the scene for many millennia. I doubt that there has been a civilisation in which they have not existed in some form.

Human beings are essentially social. We seem to need to live in relationships and in community. Whether that is because we were made that way, or simply by chance have evolved that way, might not matter for this purpose. That is the way it is. Successful hermits are a rarity. It also seems to be the case that human beings find wrong easier than right, especially when the pressure is on. The result is that our history is littered with aggression, violence, injustice, and suffering. That we are here to tell the tale at all is because our race has discovered and imposed restraints on human behaviour. Some restraints are voluntary, like the adoption of a religious faith or a moral code, but most, from the earliest recorded times, are imposed by laws administered and enforced through a judicial system. This is a feature of ancient Middle East civilisations from the third dynasty of Ur (around 2000 BC), through the Hammurabi Code and the Jewish Torah, and on through the Greek states to Roman law; and that is without considering the rest of the world at all, let alone the advent of Christianity.

As we have seen when the writer of the book of Judges observed, 'in those days Israel had no King; everyone did what was right in his own eyes', he was describing neither liberty nor Utopia but anarchy. Humanity as a race cannot, it seems, survive without restraints. What distinguishes order from chaos is the presence of effective restraints. What distinguishes one society from another is the nature and extent of the restraints imposed and the manner in which they are enforced. What distinguishes tyranny from liberty is that the effective operation of restraints is oiled by law and justice, rather than by naked power and might. However one might look at it, it seems that the effective and respected administration of justice is integral to a peaceful society.

We can trace the early origins of the system we recognise in England and Wales from the reign of Henry II (1154–89). Indeed, 1189 marked the formal start of modern law, being the date 'whereof the memory of man runneth not to the contrary'.[2] Justice in mediaeval England was seen to repose in the person of the Sovereign, but Henry decided that, rather than go round the country and do it all himself, he would appoint others to do it in his name. Thus was born the Assize and the High Court judge from which our present system has developed over the last 850 years or so, through many a turbulent phase. This section of history remains important, as the High Court judge can still exercise an inherent jurisdiction based on the Royal Prerogative rather than statute. The best current example is found in the ward of court.

Historically, a ward of court was a minor who was, for that reason, unable to control or protect his person or property. The court assumed responsibility for the education, upbringing and property of the ward and would often appoint a guardian – a much used character in 19th-century fiction. Today wardship is rarely used, but, if it is, it is either where there is a gap in statutory provision,[3] or perhaps where the parental dispute is so acute that they can no longer be trusted to exercise parental responsibility unsupervised, yet it is not in the child's best interests to be removed from either of them.[4]

Now, all this is intended neither as profound history nor sophisticated jurisprudence. It is simply intended to set the scene for understanding the role and nature of the modern judge. That judge stands in a very long line in the human experience of trying to live harmoniously as social beings. The fundamental task of oiling the machine of restraint with justice remains the same. The ways in which it is done and the social context in which it works have, however, changed almost beyond recognition.

---

[2]   See Sir Thomas Littleton (1481) and Sir William Blackstone (1780).

[3]   For example, *Re W & X (Wardship: Relatives Rejected as Foster Carers)* [2003] EWHC 2206 (Fam).

[4]   For example, *T v S (Wardship)* [2011] EWHC 1608 (Fam).

There are still many who remember social conditions in the third quarter of the last century, but even so it is not always easy to grasp the extent to which our society has changed over that time. Perhaps a way to glimpse it is to imagine a judge of the Probate Divorce and Admiralty Division (for so it was) in, say, 1955 coming to sit in the Family Court of today. The Family Division itself was not created until 1971, and the unified Family Court only in 2014. Our first female judge was appointed in 1962. Our 1955 judge (male, of course) would find it all very unfamiliar, unlike perhaps the criminal judge who would still very much recognise the essential system in which he worked.

He would, I think, be shocked at what he would see as the lack of deference shown to a modern judge and, in particular, our exposure to public criticism in the media. In fact, I think judges are still generally held in good standing but in those more deferential days, and especially when out on the Assize, they went in the name of the king and were treated accordingly.

He would, though, be astonished at the powers possessed by the modern judge and the area over which those powers now range. His family law experience would have been essentially limited to private family disputes over divorce, money, and sometimes children. He would have seen his role as a decision-maker applying the agreed norms of society to the facts as found, thus producing a just result.

In the area of private and family life, it would still have been possible in 1955 to have spoken meaningfully of the agreed norms of society. That is not to say that everyone conducted their lives accordingly (they certainly did not), but there was a broad social consensus in favour of marriage, against divorce, in favour of conceiving children in wedlock and their being brought up by both their natural parents. To talk today of the agreed values of society in this area involves much chasing after the wind. They simply do not exist in so clear a form. Judges have been significantly involved in absorbing and reflecting both change and the wide diversity in our society which is being fuelled by developing concepts of rights, medical technology, immigration, and birth control. Indeed, they have sometimes been, if not always willingly, the instigator of change.

Our 1955 judge would have been equally astonished at the range of cases which confront the modern judge in this area, including medical cases (often addressing issues of life and death) and the rapidly developing choices inherent in the concepts of welfare and best interests both for children and adults. Perhaps his greatest surprise would lie in the range of discretionary powers now given to judges. These powers fall to be exercised once the evidence has been heard, the facts determined and the relevant law identified and applied. In a complex world not only has the range of issues increased, but so also has the choice of ways to confront those issues, and thus there may be more than one 'just and reasonable' outcome available. These discretionary powers both allow the judge to make a specific decision and to serve the welfare of children or the best interests of the incapacitated adult to achieve a just solution in an individual case. The capacity of humanity to produce a set of circumstances never foreseen by the legislator is well known, and, in our society, this is met by the exercise of judicial discretion based on the rather general principles specified in the legislation.

The dramatic advance of technological skills, especially in the field of medicine, now means that society is confronted by problems it has never dealt with before. Whereas 40 years ago infants either survived or died soon after birth from natural causes, now the skills of clinicians in specialist Intensive Care Units can preserve physical life in almost all circumstances; babies die only when treatment is actually withdrawn. Something similar can happen to delay the onset of death in the older age group. Our ability to sustain physical life has meant having to make choices of how and when to end it by the refusal or withdrawal of treatment or other approaches. Developments in reproductive technology pose similar problems. When the first international commercial surrogacy cases came before the court (and they were all listed before me), it was necessary to work out how to apply a statute to a state of affairs almost certainly never considered by the legislators. Our difficulties are increased by the apparent fact that our technological skills outstrip our ethical ones; we know what we *can* do, but we are less sure as to what we *ought* to do. Judges, too, have found themselves firmly on the horns of this dilemma. When, for example, dealing with conflicts between policy and medical possibility in surrogacy cases and between life sustaining medical treatment and the futility of that treatment for the individual patient.

It is in these highly technical and often emotive cases that the role of the judge is sometimes brought into question. Judges are qualified neither in medicine nor child development, let alone specifically in paediatrics. How is the judge to decide between competing expert views? Surely it would all be better left to a tribunal of suitably qualified 'experts'?

I want to suggest that there are three reasons why the judge is better placed than anyone else to make these decisions. First, judges are skilled at evaluating contentious expert evidence and, in particular, in evaluating what is truly impartial expert evidence. Take the example of baby shaking (to which we will have to return): there are a group of experts who simply do not believe that shaking can cause the symptoms most others associate with it. On the other hand, there are experts who seem to see shaking around every corner. Evaluation of expert evidence is in these circumstances very difficult, and is best done by someone who has had an opportunity to hear and consider all the available evidence in the case, whether expert or not. Experts are human too, and have prejudices and fallibilities like everyone else.

Secondly, most of these decisions are not simply an 'expert' view. For example, when dealing with the withdrawal of treatment from a baby, there are the parents' views to consider: the judgment is a 'human' one and not just a technical one.

Thirdly, and perhaps most importantly, a just society needs the means by which a binding and authoritative resolution can be given both to disputes between citizen and citizen and between citizens and the state. The more complex and diverse our society, the more pressing is such a need.

Judges are given the status, independence and authority by society to do just that. They generally act in public (or, at least, their judgments are publicly available), and they set out their reasoning which can and should be considered, discussed and challenged in the public square. I am called the Honourable, given a knighthood on appointment and addressed as 'my Lord' not because I crave it – much less because I deserve it – but because my essential social purpose is to bring finality to disputes by a binding and authoritative decision.

This has all come under closer scrutiny since the European Convention on Human Rights was incorporated into our domestic law in 2000.[5] It is the duty of the judge to ensure that every public body (including the court) respects the human rights of the citizen. Generally, the identifying of rights is fairly straightforward. What is difficult is the resolving of conflicting rights. Almost every family case infringes someone's right to family life, as does the making of a care order in respect of the child or the reception of an unwilling adult into a care home; of course, nowhere is this more clearly seen than in the making of a contested adoption order. The resolution of these issues of conflict rests on less sure foundations than many would like, as the conflict between family life and free speech will, I believe, illustrate.

---

[5]   The Human Rights Act 1998.

A mother (as I had found in care proceedings) had killed her son in hospital by poisoning his food with salt. She was subsequently arrested and charged with murder. The surviving child had been placed with his father. I was asked to restrain the freedom of the press to report the criminal trial so as to protect the child's right to privacy. A clear choice had to be made between conflicting rights of free speech (art 10) and personal privacy (art 8). I refused to prevent the reporting. The Court of Appeal unanimously held that I had wrongly analysed the conflicting rights but, by majority, that I had got the right actual answer.[6] The House of Lords said that my analysis was correct, but one answer was wrong; however, that did not matter and the decision was upheld.[7] It really is not as easy as it sometimes seems!

The House of Lords decided that the correct approach was effectively to weigh up the pros and cons under each article and then to strike 'a fair balance'. This is the concept of 'proportionality', which is much considered today. So there you are: the trial judge has the final say. That may be all very well in the contested court case; indeed, it may be the only practical approach whether we like it or not. It does, however, have the disadvantage of making it difficult for lawyers to advise confidently on the potential outcome of the case. Given that we as a society want as few as possible of our disputes to end up actually getting to court and being decided by judges, this uncertainty is a difficulty even though it may have enabled a judge to do justice in the individual case. We will meet this tension between certainty and fairness again.

Another tension to have come under scrutiny is that between public justice and the privacy of those personal affairs being addressed in the case. Traditionally, family decisions and cases

---

6   *Re S (Identification: Restrictions on Publication)* [2003] EWCA Civ 963 on appeal from [2009] EWHC 2858 (Fam).

7   [2004] UKHL 47.

involving those who lack capacity to make their own decisions were heard in private in deference to the personal and sensitive nature of the subject matter. It was a well-recognised exception to the general rule that justice is done in public, as laid down by the House of Lords in 1913.[8] However, as society has become more complex and the powers of the judge correspondingly wider, there has been a real public interest in knowing what these powers are and how, when and why they can be exercised.

There are real merits in all cases being heard in public. It means that the public is more aware of the increasing powers vested in judges and is able to comment on, criticise and challenge them. It is, it must be said, also much easier for judges, whose reasoning is there for all to see, rather than the reporting depending on versions given by disappointed litigants. Also, there can be no 'secret court' accusations. On the other hand, the courts are dealing with some of the most intimate aspects of private life, and one can sympathise with families and children who do not want their private affairs subject to public exposure. The modern tendency, which I would very much endorse, is to open the court to scrutiny but to preserve the anonymity of the actual parties; the emphasis is thus less on who attends (provided that we do not allow parties to have rival groups of supporters in court) than on what may be reported.

A leading case on this involved a severely disabled young man who had a remarkable, and publicly acclaimed, musical talent.[9] Because of the severity of his disability, the court had to make decisions about his welfare and property which effectively touched on every aspect of his life. Clearly there were matters that should not be subject to public exposure; equally clearly, there were questions which reasonable members of the public might have which should be publicly addressed. There were

---

8   *Scott v Scott* [1913] AC 417.

9   *Independent News Media v A* [2010] EWCA Civ 343, on appeal from [2009] EWHC 2858 (Fam).

technical legal arguments in the case, but in the end it was about striking a fair balance between legitimate confidentiality and legitimate public interest, which was resolved by allowing the media to attend but imposing restrictions on what could be reported.

There is no doubt that this is a developing area of the law and that any approach involves a compromise between competing and perfectly legitimate rights. At the end of the day, Parliament must have the final say in this as they have, for example, on the question of televising courts. The courts belong to society and not to the judges. However, on a day-to-day basis, the judges are responsible for managing this tension between transparency and respect for personal privacy. In ancient Rome they achieved transparency by simply building their courts with no walls, but in our country both climate and concern for privacy are against that. However, the tension between transparency and privacy remains.

In one sense the televising of courts is doing no more than taking the walls of the building away again. We know from experience, however, that it is much more than that. Appellate hearings can now be televised, and that is to be extended to sentencing remarks in the Crown Court. Although the principal anxiety lies in not intimidating witnesses or identifying jurors, it also lies in people disrupting the process for their own reasons or simply playing to the gallery. No doubt in 10 years' time we will be in a very different place, just as we are now from where we were a decade ago. This truly remains a work in progress.

The powers of the modern judge may be both extensive and extending and should be the subject of public debate. However, these powers only come after consideration once the facts are known. It is therefore necessary to give some thought to that process where the facts themselves are in real dispute.

Chapter 3

What is Truth? The Relationship between Truth, Proof and Justice

What is the purpose of a trial or enquiry? Surely it is to get to the truth; that is why we have them. This is, of course, a proper and legitimate, indeed essential, aspiration for any society – but is it attainable? That is the question on which we must concentrate. Truth is a difficult concept. Objective truth undoubtedly exists. The universe has its origins, its composition and its destiny, as do we. The difficulty lies not in acknowledging that, but in accessing the truth that lies behind it. In a much more modest and mundane context, the same difficulty confronts the judge.

Our system, like almost every other system before, is (as we have seen) so constructed that fallible judges hear and consider fallible evidence often given by very fallible witnesses. We should not be surprised that getting to the truth is easier said than done. Pontius Pilate's question to Jesus, 'What is truth?' might be a much better one than he ever realised. At the same time, however hard we press the question of obtaining the truth, no society should abandon that aspiration as the object of the trial.

The case is over. The witnesses have all been heard, the documents read and counsel listened to; all now eagerly await the coming judgment. Young barristers are often disappointed to discover that what is troubling the judge is not their learned submissions on the law, but the dispute over what actually happened. It is at this point that the criminal judge breathes a sigh of relief and passes the baton onto the jury. As no research into jury deliberations is permitted, we can only guess at how they go about it. In all other cases, however, the judge must decide the facts. How, then, do they go about it? I am, again, not sure that there is much research on that.

Our tradition puts a significant emphasis on seeing and hearing the witnesses, thereby acknowledging that in decision-making there is a real impressionistic and intuitive element. I have certainly found that to be so, and it is not always easy for the judge to explain why one witness has been accepted rather than another, other than to say that, after reflection, the evidence of one is preferred to that of the other – an explanation that the appellate courts have made clear is acceptable.

I can only really tell you how I go about it, certainly rejecting the approach of an elderly magistrate some 40 years ago who said, only half-jokingly, 'I look at their fingernails, dear!'. Mine is an approach that I commend to new family judges through my continuing association with the Judicial College. I will try to explain the approach in the context of a care case in which the parents are said to have brought about a child's death by shaking. Sadly, it is not an allegation unknown to me; it is both emotive and controversial, but serves to illustrate the process.

The first step is promising. A large part of the evidence in any case is usually agreed, or at least uncontroversial. I begin by assembling that evidence to see whether (as is often the case) it offers both context and background to the case, and even an indicator of where the probabilities might lie. Thus, it is accepted that the child was at home when she suddenly became ill. The parents had been having a hard time with sleeping and feeding, but had regularly taken the child to the clinic without adverse comment. The child had promptly been taken to hospital but, despite best efforts, had died. The post-mortem examination had found a particular triad of injuries often associated with the shaking injury, but not itself diagnostic of it. Had the child been shaken? If so, was it whilst in the care of the parents, and, if so, who had done it? Controversial matters have to be assessed in the context of the agreed evidence. In this case, there will be one or two people who actually know the truth but the judge will not be one of them.

The judge must then make an assessment of the witnesses: are they honest, are they accurate, are they reliable? It may surprise you to know that, even after 30 years of listening to witnesses, I still start with the assumption that I am being told the truth, in the sense that what the witness is telling me is what he believes to be true.

There are perhaps three common indicators of dishonesty: evidence that is tinged with malice, evidence that is inconsistent with the agreed background, and evidence that is inconsistent with what that witness has said before. So one parent blaming the other for shaking when there is a deeply acrimonious separation and a dispute over other children will inevitably ring alarm bells. Evidence of supposed calm deliberation and reaction when the background demonstrates a chaotic family life may do likewise, as may an account given to the court which is at serious variance with what first had been said in the ambulance or at the hospital. None of these matters proves dishonesty in a particular case, but they cause those bells to ring. Even if the judge concludes that the witness is dishonest, it is important to ask why. Usually it will be to cover up a personal wrongdoing, but it may be in fear of reprisal, or a desire to protect another or even simply an inability to recognise that something is seriously amiss with their parenting.

A conclusion, however, that the witness is honest is only the start of the process. They may be honest, but are they accurate and reliable? I heard of an interesting piece of research done in which innocent bystanders were shown a video of a car crash and then asked to describe it. The variations were such that one questioned whether they had been watching the same video. I have listened to honest parents describing family life, but whose perceptions were so fixed and blinkered that I wondered whether they had really lived in the same household. You may get the truth, even nothing but the truth, but the whole truth is something of a rarity. However, at the same time, the parents' account of how the baby became ill may fit into the context of the undisputed evidence and give a real clue – for instance, that they were seriously under pressure at the time.

It is at this point that the judge has to factor in the expert evidence. This was considered in the previous chapter, but that too must be evaluated in the individual case before the judge can decide what, if any, light it sheds on the issues that need to be decided, especially where such evidence does not speak with one voice or is, as may happen, tainted by prejudice or bias.

Throughout this process, it is necessary to bear in mind the real distinction between an honest and a reliable witness. An honest witness may be very convincing but also very mistaken. The classic case is identification. I may be utterly convinced that I saw X hit Y, only for it to be discovered that X was in Australia at the time; it was just someone who looked very like X, or perhaps I had expected to see X there. We have all made a mistake of this type, sometimes with embarrassing results, but also, because we are honest and convinced, we may nevertheless give a very convincing account.

There may be a further complication: a prominent modern example is an allegation of historic sexual abuse. I have had to try many of these cases both as a criminal and a care judge, and they present considerable difficulty. We know that these allegations can take a long time to materialise. They are suppressed in the hope of being forgotten, or they simply cannot be faced, or out of fear that they will not be believed, or because they continue under the influence of the abuser. It is not unusual in my experience in family cases for allegations first to be made when a person realises that their own child may now be at risk.

There are obvious difficulties in assessing accuracy when witnesses are describing events that are said to have happened up to 50 years ago. The central event may be clear enough but even that, if continuously relived in the mind, may itself become distorted; certainly, all the surrounding circumstances are likely to have faded or become confused. The position of the person accused, if innocent, is even more difficult since they can often do little more than just deny the allegation. Their evidence will be just the same as that of the guilty party because, in many cases, abusers will have taught themselves to believe the denial and thus may appear convincing. It is, of course, right that the guilty should be held accountable. It is also right that every accused person should have a fair trial.

So all the evidence has been assembled and considered. Now the judge must turn to the disputed question. Was this baby shaken? Was this person indeed abused when young? If so, by whom? Sometimes the answer is obvious, all the evidence points one way and the outcome is not in doubt. However, that is not how it seems at this stage in most cases.

It is now that we encounter the concept of proof which is, of course, itself a creation of human thought. It applies much more widely than in the courtroom. The scientist in propounding a theory uses it. Newton's laws of motion were accepted as true because they explained the evidence – at least, they did so until the sub-atomic world was uncovered, where things happen very differently. Now, we do not abandon Newton because his laws still explain all that we can actually see; but his laws are not the whole truth. We are content to accept something that explains what we see even if it is not absolute truth, and that is rather the position we find ourselves in, in the courtroom.

The actual task laid on the judge is to determine what has been proved. The burden of proof usually lies on the one who asserts. The Crown in a criminal case, the local authority in a care case must prove that the baby was shaken, and, if so, that it was at the hands of one or both of the parents. However, at that point the criminal and civil jurisdictions divide sharply over the standard of proof. In a criminal case a person may not be convicted unless (in the modern phrase) 'the jury is sure of guilt' or (in the more traditional phrase) 'the jury is satisfied beyond reasonable doubt'. In a criminal trial the focus is on the alleged guilt of the defendant: did he do the act with which he is charged? Thus, a verdict of not guilty may carry quite different messages, ranging from 'he is innocent' through to 'we think it likely he did it but we can't quite be sure'. Because the jury gives no reasons, no one knows where on that spectrum a verdict actually lies: all it establishes is that they were not sure that the presumption of innocence had been rebutted.

The position in a civil case is quite different. There proof is only on the balance of probabilities. There is no doubt that this child died: is it more probable than not that she was shaken? If so, is it more probable than not that this was done by a parent and, if so, which or both? It is not a case of 'am I sure she was shaken' or 'am I sure which parent did it'. This has been spelt out with remorseless logic by Lord Hoffman, in a 2008 House of Lords case:[1]

> 'If the legal rule requires a fact to be proved (a fact in issue) a judge or jury must decide whether or not it happened. There is

---

[1]   *Re B (Children)* [2008] UKHL 35.

no room for a finding that it might have happened. The law operates a binary system in which the only values are 0 and 1. The act either happened or it did not. If the tribunal is left in doubt, the doubt is resolved by the rule that one party or other carries the burden of proof. If a party who bears the burden of proof fails to discharge it, a value of 0 is returned and the fact is treated as not having happened. If he does discharge it, the value of 1 is returned and the fact is treated as having happened.'

The result in the family court is this: the case must be managed in the future (and the future of the surviving children decided) on the basis that the dead child was or was not shaken and was or was not shaken by a parent, depending on whether that fact was proved or not. Thus, in a shaking case, if the parents are found culpable in the death, the future of surviving and yet to be born siblings must be decided on that basis; if not proved, the children's future must be decided on the basis that the parents were without blame for causing the deaths.

One of the reasons for the difference in the standard of proof is the consequence of error. In a criminal case the convicted defendant will go to prison but, if acquitted, will be freed. It has long been a principle in our society that it is better that the guilty be acquitted than the innocent convicted. That is why there is such a high standard of proof.

The purpose of the family hearing is, however, the protection and welfare of children. Of course, if parents are wrongly found to have shaken or abused their children, they are likely to lose them to adoption by strangers. That would be a very serious injustice, as the media have from time to time rightly pointed out. However, if wrongly they are found not to have shaken the child when in fact they had, then surviving siblings, and the yet to be born are exposed to grave risk and danger. We have sadly seen recent examples of that too. The Supreme Court has pointed out that there is a real danger either way, something that hardly has to be impressed on the anxious trial judge.

One consequence of this is that exactly opposite results on identical evidence may logically and lawfully be reached in a criminal and family court. The jury may not have been sure that the baby had been shaken, or been shaken by the person charged before them, and thus returned a verdict of not guilty. On the selfsame evidence a judge may conclude in care proceedings that the child was shaken and that the parents were culpable because that was the most probable explanation of the evidence. Indeed, in one case of alleged indecent assault by a stepfather on a teenage girl, I presided at the criminal trial where the jury acquitted but, in the subsequent family proceedings, which I tried with the consent of all parties, I found that such an assault had occurred. I could well understand why the jury would not be sure but, for me, an indecent assault was the most probable explanation of the evidence.

Now, all this is perfectly logical to a lawyer, although one suspects it may not be to everyone, or indeed anyone, else. I have expressed the view in reported cases that there ought to be consistency at least to the extent that a jury should not be invited to convict where a family court has declared the allegation unproved. However, the Court of Appeal, comprising both the then Lord Chief Justice and President of the Family Division, has made it clear that that view is wrong,[2] although they did recognise the need for close liaison between the two sets of proceedings. The criminal and care systems are wholly separate, and what is decided in one cannot be binding on the other. That clearly is now the law and we must live with what many may see as this rather puzzling paradox of different lawful conclusions based on the same evidence.

This, of course, raises the question: what is the relationship between truth and proof, and how does that relate to any acceptable concept of justice? In the examples I have given, it is

---

[2]   *R v Levey* [2006] EWCA Crim 190.

simply not possible for both results, however sound in law each may be, to be the truth. I have to say that that is an inescapable dilemma. We trust that if the matter is proved, it will be true. Indeed our system is only politically and morally acceptable on that basis. We know, however, that if something is not proved, it does not mean to say that it has been shown to be untrue; it simply has not been proved.

In order to confront the dilemma of proof and truth, we need to set our consideration in the wider context of social justice. The purpose of the judiciary is to bring finality to disputes between citizens or between citizens and the state by the giving of a final, binding and authoritative decision. Judges are not there to discuss, speculate or lecture, but to decide. The judge who fails to decide fails in his most basic social function. We have seen that our system is constructed on the basis of fallible judges evaluating fallible evidence given by all too often fallible witnesses. I trust that that assertion at least has been made good. It is also the case that, whoever might know the actual truth of a particular fact, it will not be the judge. The combination of those factors – the need for the decision, the fallibility of the process and the elusiveness of the truth – means that the whole process is very seriously and inevitably open to error: social justice is human, but would any society want it otherwise and, indeed, what alternative might there be?

It is sometimes tempting to assert that discovering the truth, something which we all too often have to do, is just a matter of common sense. Would that it were so! Human experience, however, teaches that human ingenuity is almost limitless when it comes to skewing human relationships and making human life difficult. Any family judge will have long lost count of the cases in which the facts, if tendered to a publisher of novels, would be rejected as beyond belief. Human life is often much more complicated than the imagination of the novelist allows: truly, truth is often stranger than fiction.

This dilemma confronts every new judge, and reinforces the view that the two qualities most needed by the family judge are humility and confidence. Humility is essential once it is appreciated that the system is inherently fallible, and humility requires courage: the courage to acknowledge that, however hard we try and however conscientiously we apply ourselves, we are bound to get some cases wrong. I have heard myself saying to new judges that if you can't hack the idea of getting a case wrong, this is not the job for you. What is more, we will rarely, if ever, discover which ones they are. At the same time each judge needs confidence: how otherwise can decisions be made? My method has been to approach each case with humility, decide each case with confidence and then sleep well so that it can be done, as it has to be, again and again.

Truth is foundational to justice, but so is the resolution of disputes. The job can only be done with the human tools that we have. Thus if it is better to do the job than abandon it, society may have to accept, in answer to the basic question raised, that the pure whole truth is not always accessible. It was surely in recognition of this that the concept of proof was first devised. Proof is a protection against human error and a recognition that we cannot directly read the hearts, minds and consciences of those who appear before us. In ancient civilisations – Jewish and Roman would be good examples – it was very difficult to obtain the conviction of a freeman if the prescribed due processes were in fact observed. There is nothing new about this problem: read the *Mishnah* or the *Talmud*; read Cicero.

We have certainly made matters more difficult for ourselves by having differing standards of proof. There again, we value both the presumption of innocence and the protection of children, and they do not always pull in the same direction. Those are indicators as to why we have two standards, though of course there will be others.

Could this all be done better? Of course the answer must be 'yes', and we need to ensure that proof and truth more exactly coincide. However, the inherent contradictions and fallibilities of our judicial system, not to mention the activities of those who for their own reasons are anxious to evade the truth, probably mean that things cannot be done radically differently. Society commits to judges both great power and great responsibility in the individual case, and does so in what should be the full knowledge of the inherent fallibility of any human system of justice. Thus, if as a society we are to have a politically and morally acceptable system, we must have an uncorrupted, well-trained, and independent judiciary who enjoy the trust of that society. That is the issue that underlies this book, and we shall return to it again.

Chapter 4

The State and Family Life: Should the State Intervene to Protect?

The Englishman's home is his castle and his personal liberty is his inalienable right, which he may defend by force if necessary (in an old case, by clothes prop and milk bottle) against any unlawful invasion by the state or indeed by anyone else contrary to his consent. It has been so acknowledged in our law since Magna Carta and reinforced by the European Convention on Human Rights, now part of our domestic law. So far, so good – but note the key word 'unlawful'.

In our increasingly complex society there are ever more of those who are entitled lawfully to intervene in our private life: the police and security services, social welfare and mental health agencies, and all manner of enforcers of debts and penalties. They all require official sanction from clear statutory words and many may require a court order, too. Nevertheless, considerable powers are vested in many agents of the state and are used on a daily basis. It raises an essential tension between personal liberty and the proper activities of the state, as can be clearly illustrated by a consideration of ECHR, Art 8 entitled 'Right to respect for private and family life'.

Article 8(1) says this: 'Everyone has the right to respect for his private and family life, his home and his correspondence'. That is fairly clear; but there is more, for this is a qualified, not an absolute, right. Article 8(2) provides: 'There shall be no other interference by a public authority with the exercise of this right except such as is in accordance with the law and is necessary in a democratic society in the interests of national security, public safety or the economic well-being of the country, for the prevention of disorder or crime, for the protection of health or morals, or for the protection of the rights and freedoms of others.' Those are very wide grounds indeed allowing the curtailment of the basic right. They have two built-in safeguards: first, it must be in accordance with the law; and secondly, it must be necessary in a democratic society for those listed purposes. The first is protection against arbitrary executive action and has been part of our common law for centuries. The second, however, employs the concept of 'proportionality', which we have already met. To be necessary it must not only be lawful and for the set purposes, but the invasion must be proportionate to what is to be protected or achieved. We saw how that comes down to striking a fair balance in the individual case, ultimately a judicial function.

Inevitably, therefore, private liberty and state power exist in a permanent tension in our society. My purpose here is to explore the role of the judge, in particular as gatekeeper and regulator in the holding of that tension, and I want to do so through the prism of both the Family Court and the Court of Protection. There are, of course, many other areas, notably the jurisdiction of the Administrative Court and the remedy of judicial review. I have chosen this particular approach for three reasons. First, these are areas that have seen a significant growth in judicial power over the time that I have been a judge. Secondly, they frequently generate considerable public feeling. Thirdly, they happen to be the areas best known to me in my own judicial experience.

Public feeling, like public policy, can be an unruly horse. In the aftermath of disasters like Victoria Climbié and Baby Peter, there is a clarion call: this must never happen again. It is, of course, an entirely fair reaction. It is accompanied (fuelled usually by both the media and politicians) with demands that heads should roll and enquiries be held. And enquiries have often established that heads should indeed roll. On the other hand, similar public invective is again generated (and equally fairly so) when there are interventions where there should not have been: sexual abuse in Cleveland and ritual abuse in Orkney spring to mind. I do not question either the fairness or genuineness of such reactions, but it does make understandable the feeling of those in the front line of damned if you do and damned if you don't, which is not good for morale.

On the other hand, there have always been, and always will be, adults who contrive to abuse children, whether their own or otherwise, and to conceal that abuse from others. However good our systems, no state can guarantee that this will never happen again. Moreover, the decision on the ground whether or not to intervene will take place in the heat of conflicting human emotions, and will inevitably sometimes be wrong. Hindsight is a wonderful aid to decision-making, but one that is denied both to those on the ground and to judges. We can only offer our best shot, not a guarantee of infallibility.

Now, this tension is quite legitimate as well as probably inevitable in a complex democratic society. We all prize our personal freedom and we resent our lives being nannied by the state. On the other hand, we do want a humane and civilised state able and willing to protect those not able to protect themselves and, moreover, we want a state willing and able to do that whether or not their family wanted or asked for it. Hence, we see not only the tension, but also the source of conflict of opinion.

It is the non-consensual acts that are inevitably the most controversial, but also often the most necessary. Social work intervention to remove the child at risk may be a life-saving act, just as the contrary decision may be life-threatening – not an easy balance, which comes inevitably with a tendency to err on the side of caution: you can return an unharmed child to the family if the decision to remove was wrong. The same may be true of removing an elderly person with dementia from their family to a care home. On the other hand, one of the consequences of protective intervention for a child, adoption, cannot realistically be undone. Any mistake there becomes set in legal concrete. And yet, in spite of all this (or perhaps because of it), we broadly all agree that a modern democratic society needs to have these compulsive powers.

We have noted the two essential safeguards of liberty: lawfulness and proportionality. Lawfulness in modern times will essentially derive from a statute, and that may well have further safeguards built into it. Let us take the Children Act 1989 and the Mental Capacity Act 2005, which are both foundational statutes. It is the Children Act that empowers the state to intervene in private family life by the taking of care proceedings. Of course there are many procedural requirements, but there are two substantive requirements. The first is found in s 31(2):

'A court may only make a care order ... if it is satisfied –

(a)   that the child concerned is suffering or is likely to suffer significant harm; and

(b)   that the harm or likelihood of harm is attributable to –

(i)   the care given to the child, or likely to be given to him if the order were not made, not being what it would be reasonable to expect a parent to give to him; or

(ii)   the child being beyond parental control.'

These have become known as the 'threshold criteria', in that they comprise a factual threshold that must be established before the court can intervene. That means that, unless the harm suffered or anticipated can properly be described as 'significant' and that that is attributable to want of reasonable parental care, the state has no power to intervene compulsorily. The emphasis in practice is usually on the nature of the harm involved. It is not every incident of harm that warrants intervention. I take the liberty of quoting some words of my own; partly because they are reported, partly because they have acquired widespread acceptance, and partly because they have now been expressly approved by the Supreme Court:[1]

> 'It follows inexorably ... that society must be willing to tolerate very diverse standards of parenting, including the eccentric, the barely adequate and the inconsistent. It follows too that children will inevitably have both very different experiences of parenting and very unequal consequences flowing from it. It means that some children will suffer disadvantage and harm, whilst others flourish in an atmosphere of loving security and emotional stability. These are the consequences of our fallible humanity and it is not the provenance of the state to spare children all the consequences of defective parenting. In any case it simply could not be done ...
>
> (51) ... Significant harm is fact specific and must retain the breadth of meaning that human fallibility may require... It is clear that it must be something unusual; at least something more than the commonplace human failure or inadequacy.'[2]

I hope that extract will make it clear that it is only in a small minority of families that the state will be able to establish its right to interfere. If it does not, it has no compulsive powers and must rely on parental co-operation to enlist help.

---

1   *In the Matter of B (a Child)* [2013] UKSC 33.

2   *Re L (Care: Threshold Criteria)* [2007] 1 FLR 2050.

Most people who go into social work, medicine, and allied professions as well as those who practice in these areas of the law tend to have finely honed protective instincts. We do not find it easy to see and tolerate avoidable harm. However, because there must necessarily be legal restrictions on compulsive powers, that is just what they may have to do. The concept of SureStart in deprived areas was very sound, and yet too often their proffered services were accessed by those who needed them less and spurned by those who needed them more. Child welfare is never a comfortable place to be.

A second safeguard exists, namely that the welfare of the child must be the court's paramount consideration. That is the subject of the next chapter; for now, we are concerned simply with the right to intervene in private life.

The Mental Capacity Act also has a two-stage approach. The second is the requirement to act in the best interests of the protected person, and again we will come to that in the next chapter. Our concern now is the basis on which that duty depends: namely, that the person lacks capacity to decide the specific matter in question. This question of capacity is fundamental, for, unless incapacity is established, the state has no right or power to intervene, save in those cases where mental ill-health brings a person within the limits of the Mental Health Acts. It is worth noting that, unlike the Children Act, this Act has no factual threshold that needs to be crossed.[3] Where the person concerned lacks capacity to take the decision under consideration, best interests alone dictate the outcome.

It was 10pm on a Sunday night and I happened to be the judge on call. I was rung by an A&E consultant who had admitted an elderly gentleman. The man had attempted suicide but failed, having not taken enough tablets. He needed to be washed out: if

---

[3]   *G v E* [2010] EWCA Civ 822.

he were, he would fully recover but, if not, he would die. The patient was refusing all treatment. What was to be done? The only question, as it appeared to me, was the patient's capacity to take that decision. A member of the family was willing to speak to me. It was clear that, however much the rest of the family disagreed, the patient knew what he was doing and there was no basis to find that the presumption of capacity had been displaced. Nothing could be done and he duly passed away a few hours later. Personal freedom can sometimes come at a high price, and can severely test both human love and the instinct to intervene and protect.

However, there will be many cases – many more than I think is generally believed – where the state will have power to intervene. Nowhere is that more true than among our ageing population. We now need to explore the sort of interventions that a judge may be required or empowered to authorise or, indeed, order. We therefore turn to the Mental Capacity Act 2005.

It is important to say something about capacity without trying to give an exhaustive exposition of the law. Capacity is decision-specific. There is no such thing as a person without capacity. A person can only lack capacity to take a specific decision. Crucially, a person is deemed to have capacity unless and until it is demonstrated that he lacks it; that was the key point in the hospital incident just described. Almost as important is the rule that capacity may not be inferred from an unwise decision. In practice this is significant, as it is often the taking of unwise decisions that raises questions of capacity in the first place. An unwise decision might be the result of incapacity, but it cannot be grounds for finding it. It is also important that all reasonable steps have been attempted to enable a person to take the decision.[4]

---

[4]   Mental Capacity Act 2005, s 1.

On that basis, incapacity must be due to some disturbance of the function of the brain or mind, however temporary. It must also be shown that the person concerned either cannot understand the relevant information or cannot retain it or weigh it up in the taking of the decision.[5] In practice, the emphasis on weighing up information is crucial, but it is also vital that that is not confused with failing to agree with what others see as the sensible course.

Although the assessment of capacity does not require medical expertise, it does require very great care. It is the only gateway to the best interests powers. A finding of incapacity may have lifelong consequences where, for example, it results in the admission against the wishes of the person concerned to a care home.

Once capacity has been dealt with, the very wide best interest powers become available. That may include both property and personal welfare, and it may involve either a judicial decision or the judicial appointment of a deputy to take those decisions. The most controversial decisions tend to lie in the field of where to live and with whom to associate, or in the field of medical treatment. It is important to remember at all times that the court's powers depend on incapacity and that the powers are decision specific.

I had a case of a very wealthy older man in the early stages of dementia.[6] There were many disputes within the family arising out of his desire to marry his carer. In fact, he had capacity to decide on marriage and where to live, intermittent capacity to make a will or deal with powers of attorney, but no capacity to manage his own affairs. The court could only intervene where incapacity to make a particular decision was demonstrated. The problem of having capacity for some important decisions and

---

[5]   MCA 2005, ss 2-3.

[6]   *A, B and C v X & Z* [2012] EWHC 2400 (COP).

not for others, or of having capacity to make a particular decision on some occasions but not on others, can produce real problems for carers and their advisers. It may mean, for example, that a person in this position who wants to make or alter a will may need evidence of his capacity to do so when he actually does it. An increasingly ageing population is likely to make this sort of problem common rather than exceptional.

The court has power to commit a person to a care home without their consent and against the wishes of their family, provided that it is in their best interest so to do. That, of course, involves a deprivation of liberty, and there is an administrative process (a bit like the Mental Health Act compulsory admission process) to oversee and authorise it, subject to review by the Court of Protection.[7] It is, however, a draconian power that may have lifelong consequences. The court also has power to regulate personal relationships. I dealt with the case of a young woman addicted to sex but lacking the capacity to consent to it.[8] She had consequently been badly abused. In order to protect her, it was necessary to require her to live in sheltered accommodation and only to leave it with 2:1 supervision. That is a huge incursion on privacy and liberty for someone not to blame for their own circumstances. It is also worth noting that the consequence of any such finding is that anyone who does have sexual relations with such a person commits a serious criminal offence in so doing.

Again, the court has powers to regulate medical treatment. I had to decide in respect of a seriously learning-disabled woman addicted to smoking whether she should lose a leg to extend her life, something that she would never have understood or accepted, or merely to provide palliative care.[9] Those duties are

---

[7] MCA 2005, s 21A and Sch A1.
[8] *A Local Authority v H* [2012] EWHC 49 (COP).
[9] (2010), Unreported.

entrusted to the judge by society and by statute, but how many others even know of, let alone approve of or consent to, them?

How do these things work themselves out in family law? We have already thought about how facts are determined, and we shall in the next chapter look at the concept of welfare. At present, we are concerned about the actual powers committed to the judge, rather than how or why they are exercised.

Of course the court has very wide powers to determine inter-family disputes, but those powers are effectively only exercised on the application of a family member. More controversial are the powers exercised when the state intervenes in care proceedings. One example from each set of proceedings should demonstrate the powers that exist and sometimes have to be exercised. I will start with the removal of children by one parent to another country; this is not about abduction, but removal under an order of the court.

No parent may remove the child from this country (other than for a short holiday) without the consent of all who hold parental responsibility (usually just the other parent) or permission from the court. If the removal is to be permanent, this will have serious consequences for the left-behind parent. Sometimes this arises because the resident parent has a job opportunity overseas, but more commonly these days because a parent wishes to go home. Transnational parenting is a rapidly increasing phenomenon. I have had American and Pakistani parents, English and Russian, English and Iranian, Welsh and American, and so on. They may all have lived here but, once their relationship ends, one or both of them tend to be very isolated in this country. What is to be done? The problem is most acute when the parent who wishes to leave is acknowledged to be the primary carer of the child. It is particularly difficult where the proposed country of destination does not operate under the Hague Convention, or where both parents plan to leave the country, for then the court cannot repair the consequences of its order, as it will have no jurisdiction once the child leaves the country. Not every country, or even most jurisdictions, understand child welfare as we do. The court has to assess and rely on the honesty and goodwill of parents. In a contested application, goodwill is often in short supply.

I have found that a judge needs to be very cool-headed in these cases. I asked myself what the parents would have thought would have been right had they considered the consequences of separation before conceiving the child.[10] I know that that is artificial, but it is the nearest I have got to fairness. To allow a child to go to Iran, Russia, or China may be devastating to the left-behind parent, but to condemn a child either to the loss of the primary carer or to require that carer to remain an isolated figure in a foreign country has potentially serious consequences for the child.

These cases have always been highly controversial. The courts have been criticised for paying inadequate attention to the plight of the left-behind parent and to the impact on the child or children of the loss of that parent. One has to recognise the force of that criticism, just as one has to recognise that, although parents may now use Skype and similar facilities, they are very much second-best to physical presence. The brutal fact is that parents, by freely made personal choices to become parents and then to separate, have created a situation with grave consequences for one or other of them. Of course it is never quite as simple as that, but the fact remains that, essentially, these matters are brought to a head within the family unit. These decisions simply have to be made and judges have to make them. Their ramifications can be enormous.

---

[10] For example, *S v T (Permission to Relocate to Russia)* [2012] EWHC 4023 (Fam).

We must now turn to the question of adoption, which is both politically high profile and also deeply emotive. The President of the Family Division has said that, since the abolition of capital punishment, there is no more draconian order than the removal of a child for adoption by a stranger whose identity and whereabouts are unknown to the natural parent. Yet such an order is not an unusual consequence of care proceedings today, especially where the child is very young. Its attractions for the child are obvious, and outcomes based on young placement are very encouraging. Indeed, recent research concerning a survey period of 10 years[11] shows that, where children under 4 have been placed for adoption, 97% of adoptions survived intact. On the other hand, it is difficult to envisage a more profound or devastating incursion into private family life. It is important to make two points to set this debate in context.

Adoption has been known in law around the world for centuries usually as a means of providing a male heir. However, it did not find its way into English law until 1926, and is thus but 90 years old. Its original purpose (which remained so for the first half of this period) was 'a homeless child for a childless home'. Even this was somewhat controversial, not least because our adoption law provides that an adopted person is to be treated in law as if born as the child of the adopters or adopter.[12] In more recent times, however, adoption has become an integral part of the social armoury of child protection. Hence, we find the increase in non-consensual adoptions and the feelings that that inevitably generates. Small wonder, then, that our courts, while acknowledging the place and benefits of adoption, are keen to explore all other options. Parental consent may be dispensed with where the welfare of the child so 'requires',[13] but full value must be given to that word. It is some apparent uncertainty

---

[11]   'Beyond the Adoption Order: Challenges, Intervention, Disruption'. University
       of Bristol, 2016.
[12]   Adoption and Children Act 2002, s 67(1).
[13]   Ibid, s 52(1).

about both this test for adoption and the need to explore alternatives that has caused a significant fall in the number of children currently being made available for adoption.

Furthermore, our concept of adoption is very much a minority one; not only in the world, but even in Europe. It is the compulsory extinction in law of the natural parents that runs counter to most countries' jurisprudence. The USA, Canada, Australasia and a few other countries share our view but, even among them, we hold to this view the most tenaciously, and are the ones most willing to see it through to its logical conclusion. Judges tend to be well aware of this phenomenon, not least because, increasingly, we are dealing with children from other countries and cultures who are subject to our jurisdiction because as a matter of fact they are habitually resident here, whatever their immigration status.

It is important to remember that many of those cultures do not recognise anything that approximates to the concept of adoption in English law. That does not mean that their children cannot be removed and placed for adoption, but it does mean that it may be extremely difficult to make an ethnic, cultural, and religious match for such a child. There are signs that some families from these communities are becoming willing to be adopters, but it remains to be seen how this particular question will work itself out in the future.

Adoption highlights the tension between private liberty and protection more clearly than most other issues, not least because it is final, absolute and, in practice at least, irrevocable. If the court gets it wrong either way, the implications are enormous. Children can benefit remarkably by adoption, but it comes at a very high price to the natural family. I do not believe that we have yet achieved a consensual view in our society on this, although current policy of all main political parties is very much in support of adoption.

The problem is that the concept of adoption is attractive in our society and has, at present, strong official support. The difficulty comes when the story of an individual case is told, the true loss to parents is fully understood, and the consequences of adoption laid out in specific terms. This difficulty becomes the greater if there is personal knowledge of the family, and greater still where – and this is often the case – the parents' failure to care is not culpable but, because of a lack of ability, not brought about by their own actions. These are tensions inherent in our current approach to adoption and child protection.

Consideration of the subject of intervention is not complete without a mention of the court powers in the field of medical treatment. The court has power on the application of a family member, medical authority or local authority to authorise treatment or the withholding or withdrawal of treatment, even if such an action will lead to death. How those powers are exercised is a matter of consideration in the next chapter. For the present, it is necessary just to note these powers, which may be exercised (in practice only by a High Court judge) both under the Children Act and the Mental Capacity Act and occasionally under the inherent jurisdiction, a reserve power in the High Court derived from the Royal prerogative with echoes back into mediaeval times which we noted when thinking about wardship.

These cases inevitably attract considerable public attention, as indeed they should. A requirement for a judge to decide that life-sustaining treatment should be withheld or withdrawn from child or adult is a very serious matter. Our society will see more of these cases as the medical expertise in prolonging life develops. Of course, these matters are usually resolved consensually between the treating team and the family concerned but, in the event of an unresolved dispute, a judicial decision may be needed. Once again they are considerable powers whose exercise is ultimately dictated by welfare or best interests. One asks again: how many appreciate the powers that have been committed to judges, especially the High Court judges, let alone whether they approve of or consent to them?

This whole question of state intervention in private life can find rather vivid expression in the rights of young people under 18 in respect of their own medical treatment. It highlights again this tension between private rights and the need for protection. I am aware that in academic circles this is a highly contentious issue. At present, I propose simply to describe the position as it is. All persons under 18 lack capacity in law and decisions are made for them by their parents. However, by statute,[14] a young person of 16 or above has the right to consent to medical treatment. This was enlarged by the House of Lords in the *Gillick*[15] case to include all young people who, in respect of the particular decision, met that test of capacity. However, it has always been held, on protective grounds, that they do not have the same right to refuse treatment. The young man refusing blood products, the young woman refusing treatment in the delivery suite, the young person refusing food or a course of cancer treatment are all at risk of a judge overruling their refusal on welfare grounds.

Although I think that our law as actually administered meets the specific requirements of ECHR, Art 8 and UNCRC, Art 12, I recognise that it is both controversial and, in some senses, anomalous. A child faces the full rigour of the criminal law at 10, may consent to sex at 16, may in some circumstances vote at 16, and die for their country at 17. It has to be accepted that there is a degree of arbitrariness in age limits.

I would want to defend the basic right of society to protect those under 18 from the consequences of refusing treatment. However, any such defence must begin with a recognition that the view of the young person is the starting point and should always be respected unless actually inconsistent with welfare.

---

[14] Family Law Reform Act, s 8.
[15] [1986] 1 AC 112.

There may be good grounds for refusing a transplant or another course of onerous cancer treatment. It may be perfectly reasonable to say that, as I will die sooner rather than later, I have now had enough of all this treatment. It is more difficult when the young person either may not have appreciated or may have refused to confront the true consequences of refusing treatment. The death of a child resulting from a refusal of treatment should be a decision for which some adult bears responsibility. One also has to recognise that the judges need to sleep that night too, and that is not perhaps always irrelevant in a decision to overrule a refusal.

All this may do no more than illustrate sharply that, in human life, you can never have complete rationality because we are all driven by other complex forces in addition to reason. This will become all the more apparent as we seek to explore in more detail in the next chapter concepts of welfare and best interests. But, for now, the task is to find a working balance between private rights and liberties and protection. It is the key role of the judge to be the gatekeeper of those powers whether in the assessment of the threshold criteria or the question of capacity. The judge is also the regulator of the use of those powers and the need to strike this working balance. It is essential, if that is to be accepted within society, that the judge must have the informed consent of society in so acting. It is that question that remains the fundamental concern of this book.

Chapter 5

Welfare and Best Interests: Public, Personal or Judicial Values?

The discretionary powers of the modern judge are seen most vividly – and most controversially – in the areas of child welfare and the best interests of those unable to make their own decisions. The question is: are discretionary powers compatible with justice? In his seminal work 'The Rule of Law',[1] the late Lord Bingham wrote: 'Questions of legal right and liability should ordinarily be resolved by the application of the law and not the exercise of discretion.' He concludes his chapter entitled 'Law not Discretion' with these words: '... No discretion should be unconstrained so as to be potentially arbitrary. No discretion may be legally unfettered.' As it happens, he does not discuss family or mental capacity law, but their practice, superficially at least, does not always sit easily with the principle that he identifies; one with which most would want to agree.

Now of course discretion, even in these areas, is not legally unfettered. The jurisdiction is conferred by statute, principally in Children Act 1989, s 1, Adoption and Children Act 2002, s 1

---

[1]   Published by Allen Lane (2010) and Penguin Books (2011).

and Mental Capacity Act 2005, s 4. The jurisdiction is, however, very wide, and in many cases it is the truly controversial aspect of the dispute. It is made more difficult by the fact that, although there may be more than one reasonable outcome available, one specific decision is required. These areas are deeply affected by human emotions, which may not be effectively constrained by rationality but could be seriously constrained by what is practicable. I have often thought that family law is essentially the management of the consequences of human failure so as best to protect those least able to protect themselves. That approach does not, of course, always make for consistency.

Parliament has imposed limits on discretion by providing a checklist of the matters the court is required to consider in exercising its welfare jurisdiction. These are found in the sections mentioned above; although, in the last case, 'checklist' is probably rather too narrow a description.

In respect of children, these include the views of the child together with age, gender, any specific needs they might have, and any harm they may be at risk of suffering. In adoption cases this is expanded to considering the position of the extended family and seeing all matters from a lifelong perspective of being an adopted person.

Best interests for adults is dealt with in MCA 2005, s 4. This requires a very broad perspective to be held, taking into account all the relevant circumstances (focusing in particular on the wishes, beliefs, and values of the protected person expressed while competent) together with anything else they may have taken into account themselves, as well as the views of any person interested in them. The protected person must be enabled to take as full a part in the process as they can and consideration must be given to whether, and if so when, that person may regain capacity. To emphasise the breadth of the enquiry, 'relevant circumstances' are defined as those '(a) of which the person making the determination is aware, and (b) which it would be reasonable to regard as relevant.'[2] You cannot get wider than that.

These are all matters you would expect to find. Their message is: get to know the child or protected person as well as you can. What the statutes do not do, however, is to make the lists exhaustive or to provide for any hierarchy of importance between them, let alone suggest any answers. So long as the judge has taken account of all matters mentioned in the statute, the judge decides both the priority and also the relevance of other factors. In practice the discretion, if not actually unfettered, is in truth very wide.

It is, of course, important to remember that the court cannot interfere simply because it has a view about welfare or best interests. It can only intervene either where invited by the family to do so, or where the threshold criteria of fact have been proved, or where the court is satisfied that the person lacks capacity to make the particular decision. That is the judge's role as gatekeeper. Nevertheless, that leaves a large number of cases in which the court can and is required to exercise this very wide discretion.

It seems to be the case that the concepts of welfare and best interests are interchangeable and merely depend on which statute is under consideration. In the field of medical cases the terms are indeed used interchangeably and, as the maximum age under the Children Act is 18 and the minimum age under the Mental Capacity Act is 16, it is as well that this is so. I shall use the term 'welfare' for children and 'best interests' for adults, as the statutes do, but draw no distinction in meaning between them. We are now concerned with the role of the judge as regulator of these powers.

---

[2]   Mental Capacity Act 2005, s 4(11).

Two things will have occurred to you about these concepts: first, that they are value-laden; and secondly, that they are liable to change as society changes. We have considered the position of the judge from 1955, but in fact changes can take place within very much shorter timescales: same-sex parenting and surrogacy arrangements are perhaps two obvious examples, neither of which were up for discussion when I started practice and still bordered on the unmentionable when I first became a judge in 1992. Changes happen more frequently than legislators provide, and so the modern judge has to undertake an unfamiliar role in the discernment and even formulation and development of those changes. It may be instructive to see how this works in practice.

We have seen that social values have become much more diverse in recent times just as we have seen that judges may hold between them an assorted range of values. In consequence, when the court is considering the exercise of discretion, it will often be addressing at least three potentially competing sets of values: the values of society insofar as they can be discerned; the values of the family or families engaged in this particular case; and the judge's own values, which are inevitably engaged.

These three sets of values are, in practice, quite elusive. The values of society are constantly shifting. Do the ideas represented by the term 'political correctness' represent the values of society? Are we looking for a majority view or only those views that can be described as consensual? This is a minefield, and all the judge can do is to ask, in relation to the specific question under consideration: does society essentially speak with one voice on this? The values of the family engaged may be very different from those of other families, as we will all know from our experience of living in a religiously, culturally, and ethnically diverse country. Moreover, we cannot ignore the values of the judge. It is unlikely that they will be referred to in the judgment; indeed, they may just be those cultural assumptions of which we are so often unaware or at least do not articulate. My background has presumably imbued me with assumptions that have simply become part of me and, however self-aware I try to be, I will not spot everything. That will not stop them affecting my thinking. All this must go into the welfare pot.

Let us take three examples to see how this might work. First, a family wishes to practice FGM; on that question society and the judge speak as one, and family values must give way. Take, secondly, male circumcision. I am not sure that society has a stance, although most will resist physical interference for which there is no therapeutic purpose. Judges may have strong personal views one way or the other; however, the family view may be crucial if that is the group and culture within which this boy is to grow up, and in this case it may have to prevail. Thirdly, take the physical discipline of children, a divisive issue irrespective of race, age, gender, class or culture. In those circumstances the court may not be able to go beyond requiring compliance with the criminal law. Resolving conflicts of values is often at the heart of the discretionary exercise, but it is not the whole of it.

The question of welfare may be constrained simply by what is practicable. In a family dispute the court will rarely go against a parental agreement; that is partly because we respect the rights of parents to make such agreements, even where we think we could do better, but also partly out of the recognition that it would be very difficult to enforce something else if the child is to remain at home. Discretion may have to be tempered by what is practicable. Again, a discretionary opinion based on welfare may have to be tempered by consequence. A judge found herself publicly accused of tolerating parents beating their children. That they did so was not in doubt, although they had come to recognise that their approach required change. What in fact the judge had done was to conclude that the removal of the children from their parents would, for those children, have been a yet greater evil, and should therefore not be done. This is another example of not being able to spare children all the consequences of what the adults around them choose to do. It was a case in which welfare would have to accept what it would have preferred to avoid.

Again, as ever with questions that involve human rights issues, there is the matter of proportionality to be applied to welfare. Let me take two examples from adult cases, one of which we have already seen. That related to a young woman with significant learning difficulties who was addicted to sexual activity, and had in consequence been repeatedly and seriously abused.[3] Her protection could only be secured by requiring her both to live in supervised accommodation and to be the subject of 2:1 supervision when out. But that could not be required during the whole of her sexually active life, for it would have resulted in both a cost and an intrusion grossly disproportionate to the risk, however acute that in fact was. A balance had to be struck and her best interests had to accommodate that balance, and thus these restrictions would have to be withdrawn once she had learned all that she could about self-protection. The other involved the case of a woman with significant learning difficulties who had formed a relationship with a man who was subsequently subjected to a lengthy prison sentence for the serial abuse of previous wives.[4] She married him in prison. In due course he was released on licence; his licence period expired and still she could see no risk to herself. Both wanted to resume cohabitation. The formal psychiatric advice was that she should have no contact with this man, and doubtless you can understand why. But the fact was that she was married and both wanted to cohabit: compulsory segregation was simply

---

3   *Re H* [2012] (above).
4   *CYC v PC and NC* [2012] COPLR 670. This judgment was reversed on appeal on the basis that she had capacity to make this decision.

disproportionate, and again her best interests had to accommodate that balance with such voluntary protection as could be devised.

Proportionality then not only requires the least intervention consistent with best interests, but also may sometimes require a reassessment of those best interests. The exercise of discretion involves a deeply human judgment that may not always accord with a purely rational assessment. On the other hand, best interests are governed neither by culpability nor sentiment. Of course, if parents have deliberately injured or killed a child, then the adoption by strangers of that child or surviving siblings is not a difficult outcome to contemplate. However, removal and adoption may be no less necessary where parental failure stems not from culpability, but from inadequacy or infirmity; although it may be an altogether much more difficult outcome to contemplate. Let me offer you two examples from my experience. Both come from the County Court, and therefore neither has been reported.

A single mother with a young daughter was diagnosed with Multiple Sclerosis. Gradually their roles were reversed and the child, fiercely loyal to the mother though she was, was in danger of losing her childhood. Everyone recognised that this could not go on indefinitely, but the emotional difficulties of doing anything were self-evident. In the end the girl went to her separated father, but not without a great deal of heartbreak. Again, take the case of a boy of 10 with severe Cerebral Palsy. His parents could not cope and their own siblings had their own families. His care had fallen to the grandparents, who had actually done very well; but they acknowledged that they could not care for him alone until he was 18, let alone beyond that, as he would undoubtedly need. The local authority had found an adoptive couple who would commit to him for life and the local authority argued that a decision and consequent change should be made sooner rather than later: an entirely logical argument.

In the end I refused to remove him because I believed, first, in the need to retain the good care that he had for so long as that could be done, and, secondly, that the rest of the family would rally round as the grandparental strengths failed. Was I right? I simply do not know. Best interests are not purely rational. They have an element of proportionality and, indeed, of instinct and often, as here, there was more than one reasonable answer but only one decision is allowed. This is discretion far removed from Lord Bingham's secure founding of rights in the law or, perhaps more accurately, the breadth of the human condition affected by those rights means that their actual outworking (rather than their basis) is somewhat diffuse.

One aspect of discretion that is becoming increasingly recognised is the role that the child or protected adult should have in the assessment of their own best interests. The court must take account of the wishes and feelings of the child, making due allowance for their age and understanding. The communication of those views in public law is the responsibility of the guardian and in private law of the Cafcass reporting officer, if one has been appointed. Otherwise the judge may be dependent on what the parents say, and often those parents have only been told what the child thinks they want to hear. I favour seeing children in principle where parents, guardian and child all support it, but I am very reluctant to further embroil a child in a dispute by seeing them if to do so is controversial, unless there is some special strong ground like a strongly expressed view by an older child, although even there communication by letter might be sufficient.

The official view is increasingly in favour of direct communication between child and judge. This does not have to be a face-to-face meeting. Many children would find that intimidating and most do not want physical involvement in the court process. However, where a child wants it, more judges will now be happy to meet in person. I think it difficult to insist that a judge should meet a child as, if the judge is ill at ease, the child is likely to feel the same. Letters to the judge are now encouraged, and no doubt other forms of communication will find favour too. The key issues are: does the child feel they have been heard? Does the judge fully appreciate that child's wishes and feelings?

It is very difficult to be prescriptive about these matters beyond the statutory requirement to consider wishes and feelings. It is also hard to be prescriptive about the weight to be given to those wishes and feelings. Sometimes they will be decisive, and the older the child the more this may be so. Other times, however, I suspect that an intelligent adolescent is nevertheless merely the voice-piece of one particular parent, and I will then give little weight to it. It will always be relevant, but will always be subject to the judge's overall assessment of welfare. That is most clearly seen in those cases already mentioned where a competent young person seeks to refuse medical treatment.

This question of hearing the person's voice can be more difficult in the case of an adult for there may not be an independent report involved. Section 4 of the Mental Capacity Act 2005 requires the court not only to consider his expressed wishes, but what those wishes might have been had he been competent, together with the values and beliefs that would have underpinned those views. That is a fair and healthy requirement but not always easy to discern, especially where, as is often the case, there is no written expression of any view executed while still competent. The protected person's condition may prevent any close involvement in the court process. We still have quite a way to go before we can be confident that the protected person's voice has been clearly and accurately heard. The developing role of independent mental capacity advocates promises much, but they come at a price that the state may not always be willing to pay.

If the child is to express her wishes and feelings, she needs to have accurate information and that raises the sometimes thorny question about what children know about their background. In the field of adoption we have now effectively got a consensus: the children should know all about it. A good life storybook and a willingness truthfully to answer the questions asked (but not those that have not been asked) will, in practice, meet those needs. But there remain many children conceived by IVF or as a result of a casual liaison who remain in ignorance of their genetic origins. The trouble is that, while children in the end find truth easier than fiction, the responsible adults do not always see it that way. The danger is, of course, not only may the child be expressing a view based on untruth, but that the truth will come out in some angry, uncontrolled way in adolescence, not to mention the possibility of genetically transmitted disease. All the extended family will be implicated as they will usually have been party to the withholding of the truth.

An unusual but vivid example is found in the case that I heard where a man had been convicted of sexual assault on his natural children.[5] Years later he married a woman whom he told of this, but they decided not to tell their own children. As these children grew into adolescence, the local authority discovered the position and wanted the children told so that they could self-protect. The parents refused, saying (probably with some justification) that such a revelation would be more than the children could cope with, and certainly it was more than the adults could. The question arose as to whether it was in their best interests, not least because their father had started to live apart from them and to have restricted contact at the insistence of the local authority. I decided that they should know. Although, of course, there was more than one rational outcome, the appellate courts refused to review what they saw to be a

---

5   (2011), Unreported.

typical exercise of discretion, notwithstanding the significance and the consequences of the decision.

The discretionary jurisdiction is often powerfully illustrated in the area of medical treatment, especially where a decision might have irreversible consequences. Again, let me take two examples from my experience. In one case a baby had suffered catastrophic brain injury in a domestic accident for which no one was to blame.[6] In due course the treating team concluded that any further treatment was futile, and thus all invasive treatment should be withdrawn and the child be allowed to die. Unsurprisingly the parents objected, not least on the basis that whilst there is life there is hope, as well as certain faith-based grounds. The case had to be decided on the basis that the welfare of the child should be the court's paramount consideration. That meant that preserving life was the starting point, although not necessarily the decisive one. In the end, I authorised the withdrawal of treatment and the child passed away within 24 hours. How does that square with a welfare approach? Of course, the child was never going to survive without invasive treatment and all accepted that he could not remain on it forever. In that sense premature death was inevitable. I reasoned the case on the basis of an innate human desire for a 'good death' and, while it was not easy to describe a good death for a child, it was possible to describe a bad one: isolated from all human contact whilst wired up to invasive machinery in the course of futile treatment. You will not find that reasoning in any statute or textbook; it was the exercise of the discretionary jurisdiction in welfare. Are we happy with it? Does it elicit the general consent of society at large? At least this child did have a 'good' death in the arms of the parents.

The second example involves a married woman whose four children had all been removed permanently from the care of the

---

6   *An NHS Trust v Baby X* [2012] EWHC 2188 (Fam); cf the high profile case of *Wyatt* [2004] EWHC 2247 (Fam).

parents on the grounds of complete parental incompetence. Both parents remained sexually active and committed to each other. Another child and another contested removal were, therefore, almost inevitable. The mother's learning difficulties disabled her from making decisions about pregnancy, let alone from parenting. I found it was in her best interests to have an invasive, long-term contraceptive device fitted. The reasons may be obvious, but does the existence, let alone the exercise, of such a power elicit the general consent of society?

At the heart of these issues lies the tension between protection and autonomy. While this principally affects decisions relating to adults, it is also relevant to those affecting older children. This question needs a chapter to itself, such is its importance today, and perhaps even more so tomorrow, in our society.

Sometimes welfare can conflict with public policy such as where people go overseas, enter into a commercial surrogacy agreement perfectly legally there but wholly illegal here, and then bring the child back to this country. Under the law of that country they are the legal parents; under our law the surrogate parents are the legal parents. The child is a legal orphan with no rights of residence here but nowhere else to go. In the end, it has been decided that, in the absence of fraud or oppression, the welfare of the child trumps both the illegal acts of the parents and the requirements of public policy; a parental order is made conferring parental status on them.[7] There is a real choice to be made and we have decided to allow welfare to prevail over law. Are we happy with that? And how does it sit with Lord Bingham's views? Does it elicit the general consent of society?

Interestingly, Parliament has taken a hand on this occasion. Originally these cases were dealt with under an Act of 1990.[8]

---

[7]   *Re X & Y (Foreign Surrogacy)* [2008] EWHC 3030 (Fam).

[8]   The Human Fertilisation and Embryology Act 1990.

All these issues arose whilst Parliament was reviewing that Act. No relevant change was made initially in the new Act[9] but, in Regulations made under it, the concept of welfare in the Children and Adoption Act 2002 was imported into the new Act.[10] The effect of that was to make welfare the court's paramount consideration. In consequence, it became effectively impossible to contemplate circumstances in which public policy could outweigh welfare.[11] For those wealthy enough to go abroad, the restrictions on surrogacy in our domestic law could simply be avoided.

I hope that I have been able to demonstrate the profound nature not only of the discretionary powers that judges possess, but the profound consequences of the exercise of those powers. It is not surprising that Lord Bingham urges caution over discretion. My questions are: do we know the nature and extent of these powers, and do they elicit the general consent of society?

Could we therefore perhaps inject rather more certainty into our system? The only real alternative to discretionary decision-making is to make it rule-based. Let me take two examples. The first relates to Sharia in relation to children. A Muslim English family lawyer explains it thus: 'Unlike English law, Sharia law has clearly stipulated rules as to which parent will take care of the child according to the child's age, gender, wishes and feelings and, of course, best interests. Therefore, while there are clearly defined instances when a mother has residence and when a father has residence according to Sharia, Islamic scholars are required to measure any decision they make with the yardstick of best interests.'[12] There is, therefore, a rule-based approach, but even here with the residual discretionary adjustment to be

---

9   The Human Fertilisation and Embryology Act 2008.
10   Human Fertilisation and Embryology (Parental Orders) (Consequential etc) Order 2010.
11   *Re L (Commercial Surrogacy)* [2010] EWHC 3146 (Fam).
12   *Islamic Family Law*, Raffia Arshad (Sweet & Maxwell, 2010).

made. The second example comes from family property law. English law has a discretionary system requiring a just division in each particular case whereas Scottish and much European law is more rule-based and less flexible.

A rule-based approach allows much greater certainty of advice to be given, but may produce an unjust result in the given case. While the discretionary approach may permit a just outcome in each case, it produces uncertainty that may provoke rather than quench dispute. The argument between the two will no doubt rumble on. The English tradition, at least in the field of family and mental capacity law, tends strongly towards the discretionary approach with the consequence that the law develops incrementally on a case-by-case basis.

The more I reflect on this question of judicial discretion – and I have thought much on it over the last 20 years – the more I am conscious of the power which society has put into the judges' hands, and which generally Parliament has shown no desire to curtail. The truth is that the system can only work credibly for so long as the judges receive (and, of course, deserve) the confidence and consent of the society in whose name they act. That trust must be predicated on an understanding of the nature and extent of those powers, and that is one of the principal purposes of this book. The reality is that in exercising these powers the judges are not just reflecting society, but are making an active contribution in influencing its development. That is why the matter to which we must now turn – the tension between protection and autonomy – is so important.

Chapter 6

Securing Protection or Promoting Autonomy?

There have always been those in society who have needed to be protected. The most obvious group is children; however, there are many who still have that need in adulthood. At the risk of oversimplifying, they basically fall into four categories: first, those who are mentally ill and, as their welfare is subject to the Mental Health Acts, they fall outside the ambit of this book; secondly, those with significant learning difficulties; thirdly, those with acquired brain injury (as a result of disease or accident); and fourthly, that growing group of the elderly in the various stages of dementia. Together they comprise a significant number in modern society. Our focus at present is on adults, although we shall return to the position of children later.

The history of the public protection of the vulnerable over the last few centuries in this country is not a particularly happy one, and even in the final quarter of the last century was at best haphazard, especially where the Mental Health Acts were not engaged. When a decision compulsorily to interfere with someone's liberty was finally challenged, the European Court,[1] among other defects in our system, noted the absence of any

---

[1]   *HL v UK* (Application No. 45508/99) ECtHR.

procedure as to who could authorise admission, any criteria for so doing, any means of giving reasons for so doing, any process of review, or any means of ensuring that the protected person's voice was heard – a distinctly unhappy state of affairs. By then the Mental Capacity Act 2005 had already been passed; therefore, very substantial amendments were required and were made to it in 2007 under the generic title of Deprivation of Liberty safeguards.

That process is now subject to statute, but the demands on the system continue to grow. One early question in dispute was the meaning of 'deprived of liberty'. Initially the approach of the courts was to consider what restrictions were placed on a person necessarily by reason of their disability: did they have to be kept in the house, or locked in at night, or restrained so that they could eat? If the restrictions were not increased as a result of a local authority intervention, then such people were taken as not being deprived of their liberty.[2] The Supreme Court has, however, rejected that view, insisting that deprivation of liberty means exactly what it says, however necessary or well-intentioned that might be.[3] As a result, there has been a dramatic rise in numbers of those legally deprived of liberty and who must now be dealt with in the statutory regime. Central to that regime is a requirement that any such deprivation of liberty must be in the protected person's best interests.

There is evidence that the system is in danger of being overwhelmed by the demands made upon it. The question of best interests is the one that often requires the most care and thought, and is therefore the one most at risk of a shortcut in any over-pressured system. That is a factor that has to be recognised in any reflection on what best interests should actually mean in practice.

---

[2]   *Cheshire West and Chester Council v P* [2011] EWCA Civ 1257.

[3]   Ibid, on appeal [2014] UKSC 19.

On one matter all do seem agreed: best interests must be the lodestar by which decisions to intervene, and the forms of intervention by the state, are taken. However, as we have seen, you will search statutes, regulations and decided cases in vain for a definition of 'best interests'. What we have are the provisions of MCA 2005, s 4. The key to applying that section is the perspective of the protected person himself. Artificial in some senses, and difficult though it may be in practice, the intention is to try to discover what the protected person might have decided, had he the capacity so to do. I recognise that this is a sound approach, but its inherent difficulty will be obvious.

Indeed, this approach highlights the tension between autonomy and protection. To use the perspective of the protected person allows a decision to be made which reflects what they would have decided had they been competent. That is to promote autonomy. On the other hand, the very fact that such powers exist, and may only be used so far as they secure what in the decision-maker's opinion is the best interests of the protected person, demonstrates the need for oversight and safeguarding. That is to secure protection.

It is important to note that both promoting autonomy and securing protection have very long and honourable ethical traditions. They were often articulated originally in religious language, and those who stand within faith communities often continue to use that language. Those traditions, however, have in this respect very much been absorbed into secular culture and found expression in the language of that culture.

Within the Judeo-Christian tradition each human being is seen as created by and ultimately accountable to God; that is the foundation for promoting the autonomy of each individual. The foundational thinking for what has become the modern concept of human rights was provided by the 17th-century English philosopher John Locke. His reasoning was based on the fact that, as all human beings are created in the image of God, so they have inherent rights in respect of their treatment by one another. This was thinking that found its way into the American Constitution – all are created free and equal – and so into the concept of human rights which has itself been developed since 1945. While the intellectual origins of human rights are rarely acknowledged today, the concept provides a strong ethical basis for promoting autonomy.

A similarly strong tradition of protection also exists. In the Judeo-Christian tradition there is the powerful protective emphasis on being one's brother's keeper. This is seen further in the 'Kinsman-Redeemer' in the Book of Ruth, who is obligated to support the weak in the extended family, then on through a pronounced prophetic tradition to support the weak and continued in the practice and teaching of the Christian church up until now. It has, of course, strong resonance in other religious traditions and has also been absorbed into secular thought and language and, indeed, quite often in the language of human rights; securing the protection of the vulnerable remains an aspect of human rights.

There is another tension that lies behind this desire to protect. By way of background, it is important to recognise that those who choose to work in this area are likely to both have strong protective instincts and strong personal value systems. It is important also to recognise that they work under intense pressure; not only because of actual workloads, but because this work is done under scrutiny. A misuse of power, or a mistake in exercising it, all too often provides red meat for a hungry media. With those matters in mind, we can turn to this tension: between promoting physical and emotional well-being.

Best interests is a multi-faceted concept with physical, mental, emotional, and spiritual components. In an ideal world, a best interests decision will be able to enhance all these aspects. In fact they do not necessarily all pull in the same direction, as one of the examples below will show. Someone's physical and mental protection may well be better served by being in a care home, rather than the potential squalor and awkward relationships of returning to a home where the family are struggling to hold it all together. On the other hand, if that has been the home, partner, and family of many years, then possible squalor and lack of mental stimulation may be a price worth paying for the emotional value of love, security and a sense of place and belonging, especially towards the end of life. A strong argument may be possible both ways, but only one decision is possible; thus, a choice must be made. This tension can be irreconcilable.

Now, pressure of work and exposure to criticism is likely to produce a risk-averse culture. Such a culture is always likely to prioritise physical protection because that is what can be seen and measured. In a care home, the protected person will be kept warm, clothed, fed and provided with stimulating activity. That can be seen and measured, but emotional deprivation in sadness, isolation, and the loss of sense of belonging are not readily susceptible to measurement. Likewise, at home squalor can be measured (and professionals criticised) but a sense of security cannot.

No public servant in the present climate can fairly be blamed for making physical protection a priority. However, there is a sound case for arguing that, in terms of human well-being and thus in terms of best interests, emotional protection maybe even more important. Thus, when one of these cases comes before a judge, emotional well-being may well be decisive; I certainly often thought it so. Judges are very well protected. A High Court judge can only be dismissed on an Address of both Houses of Parliament. That has not happened at least since 1689. Although a judge may be freely criticised, they are not subject to the same pressures exerted on other public servants.

With all that recognised, we can return to the fundamental
tension between promoting autonomy and securing protection.
In many cases a good best interests decision will be able to do
both. Sometimes, however, that will not be possible and choices
will have to be made. Perhaps the best way to see this at work is
to take three cases by way of example, two of which we have
met before.

We start with the case of the young learning-disabled woman
addicted to sexual activity, whose protection involved not only
living in a controlled environment but being subject to 2:1
supervision in public.[4] The promotion of autonomy would at
the very least allow the enjoyment of an active sex life, and she
did in fact have a boyfriend. The securing of protection,
however, demanded the reverse because of her total inability to
control her sex life in a safe way. A choice had to be made. Now
this choice had to take account of practicalities too, which
necessarily include cost. Best interests decisions are not abstract,
but concrete decisions involving real people in real situations
governed by real restraints. This form of protection could not go
on forever: that would be neither practicable nor proportionate.
Nevertheless, it shows the tension in play.

That can also be seen in the case of the learning-disabled
woman who wanted to live a married life with a man who had
served a long sentence for abusing previous wives.[5] The
requirements of protection could only be met by complete
separation, yet they were married and the promotion of
autonomy had to involve their living together. A choice had to
be made, but that best interests decision, too, had to be one that
was both practical and proportionate.

Our third case[6] concerns an elderly man who had effectively
wrecked his brain with alcohol but had found a home with a

---

4   *A Local Authority v H* (above).

5   *CYC v PC & NC* (above).

6   *P v M (Vulnerable Adult)* [2011] 2 FLR 1375.

widow and her adult son who, in truth, were barely able to care for him unaided, which is how they had wished to do it. Illness took him into hospital and, on his being certified fit for discharge, the unanimous professional view was that he required institutional care. However, he and the family were committed to his going 'home' where he was wanted and felt that he belonged, whatever the risk to his physical care.

This case classically illustrated both the tension between autonomy and protection and that between emotional and physical protection. The man was allowed home on the basis that his emotional welfare trumped the risks to his physical well-being. Were these decisions correct? Who knows? They were judgments based on evidence that did not all point in the same direction. They were value-laden decisions that were based on the undefined concept of best interests informed by the wide range of matters raised in s 4 of the 2005 Act. Which of those matters are decisive, or indeed whether the decisive matter is to be found in some other 'relevant' circumstance, are matters for judicial discretion, and that in practice means the discretion of the trial judge.

I think it fair to say that the courts will generally seek to promote autonomy where to do so is not inconsistent with the basic requirements of protection. The Court of Appeal[7] have said in a case involving another woman found to lack capacity to consent to sexual relations:

> 'The intention of the Act is to allow the protected person, as far as possible, to make the same mistakes as all other human beings are at liberty to make and not infrequently do.'

This is a proper illustration of both not inferring incapacity from an unwise decision, and also of promoting autonomy by allowing the protected person to get things wrong. In the field of

---

7   *IM v LM, AB and Liverpool CC* [2014] EWCA Civ 37.

personal relationships, few of us take kindly to the uninvited advice of others. Of course, this does all depend on what is meant by the words 'as far as possible'. In my opinion, they do no more than reinforce the basic principle of the Act that any decision taken on behalf of another must be one that the decision-maker is satisfied is in the best interests of the protected person. It is not the purpose of the Act to 'dress the incapacitous person in forensic cotton wool',[8] but neither is its purpose to produce a solution that does not adequately protect, just because it is what the protected person would have wanted.

In all this we cannot ignore practical restraints on action. A particular service given to one person means resources not available to someone else. A decision, logical in itself, that cannot be enforced is sometimes worse than useless: an example is where one partner has an adverse effect on the other, but both remain committed to each other – a requirement to stay apart may in practice be completely unenforceable. Moreover, the implications of fully protecting someone may, as we have seen, produce grossly disproportionate results that are morally barely defensible. All this has to be fed into the best interests decision.

Where there are tensions of the sort under consideration here, it is difficult to see how they can be resolved in individual cases without the exercise of discretion. Such decisions when made administratively can be challenged in the Court of Protection but, as we have seen, such decisions made judicially are very difficult to challenge. Yet these decisions can have lifelong implications; most people admitted into a care home do not live independently again. It raises again the basic questions about discretion canvassed in this book. Are we as a society aware of the powers which judges exercise in our name? Do these powers exist with our consent? Do judges in exercising them have (and deserve) that consent? The complexity of our society may mean

---

8   *Re P (Abortion)* EWHC 50 (COP).

that there are few serious alternatives to the existence and exercise of discretionary powers, but in a healthy democracy these questions should be raised and considered.

Before parting with the tension between autonomy and protection, we need to return to the position of the older child. The tension is plainly seen in the question of the refusal of medical treatment where, although autonomy is the starting point, protection has a real role to play. Where a child is under 16 but *Gillick*[9] competent protection may play yet a greater role, but even here the constraints of practicality must be observed. A girl of 14 gets pregnant and wants an abortion to which her parents will not consent, or the parents want an abortion but the child does not. It is very hard to visualise circumstances in which an abortion would be ordered on an unwilling woman, however much she may be unable to parent a child: how, in practice, would you actually get her to hospital and receive compliance? The other question is more difficult but, if the medical and social work opinion supports abortion, it is hard to see it being refused. I have once authorised an abortion on a woman whose severe learning difficulties meant that she understood nothing of sexuality, pregnancy, or parenthood. She had become pregnant as a result of a serious criminal offence having been committed and was refusing to co-operate in any way in a safe pregnancy. This was one of those cases in which protection, with all its problems, trumped autonomy, if only because autonomy was in those circumstances a wholly artificial concept.

The question can also arise in terms of the wishes of the child. She has sided with one parent to the exclusion of the other. How far should that autonomy be respected or does the need to protect her long-term welfare require a relationship with both parents? He has decided that he does not want to go to Australia

---

[9]   Above.

where his primary caring parent has a home or job or new partner. His wishes may seriously conflict with his needs for that carer or to remain part of the sibling group.

All these cases have to be resolved on their own facts; there are no prescribed answers. They involve balancing the promotion of autonomy with the securing of protection. That may in the end involve a choice between the two. As can be seen, the consequences of such a choice may be profound and long-lasting. They lie at the heart of the judge's discretionary jurisdiction.

So far we have concentrated on family and mental capacity law. There is, however, another area which is constantly under scrutiny and where discretionary powers, although more limited, still attract public reaction and criticism. No reflection on judicial discretion will be complete without looking at sentencing in criminal cases.

Chapter 7

Sentencing: What is Society's Purpose?

Sentencing is an emotive and controversial issue, always a potentially toxic combination, and no one knows that more acutely than the sentencing judge. Sentence in many cases, especially involving death, sex, or children is passed in a highly charged emotive atmosphere with both sets of families usually present. The emotive atmosphere can now be aggravated by statutory requirements that result in much longer sentencing remarks. It is also the one judicial function in which half the population and all the media think that they are experts too; hence, the controversial element.

It is my strong impression that the general level of sentencing has increased over the past 40 years: our prison population has doubled while the overall level of crime has decreased, and whether those phenomena are linked is a matter of intense political debate. There are many reasons for this increased sentencing tariff, including a change in the types of offences (like terrorism) that dominate the Crown Court calendar. At the present time, it appears that around 40% of Crown Court time is devoted to alleged sexual offences. I, however, want to suggest four further reasons from my own reflections.

The first is that our society has become more punitive over the last few years. Actually, I think we have reverted to type and that it was the last quarter of the 20th century, with its many experiments in reducing the use of custody, which was the exception; although its supporting voices can still be heard in public discussion. A brief look at the history of sentencing in this country reveals a deeply punitive approach. Even as the 19th century dawned, there were over 300 offences punishable by death; and transportation and whipping were common punishments for what today would be regarded as no more than offences of moderate seriousness. Those who support a different approach make the point that London then was a much more dangerous place than it is now, even if the scope for recidivism then was less. Prevention of crime does indeed depend on very much more than the current sentencing regime.

I am now convinced that the sentencing regime has little significant effect on the actual commission of crime. This is partly because most crime is instinctive or opportunistic, fuelled by drink or the need for drugs, in which the one thing that never crosses the offender's mind is the consequence of being caught. Deterrence is of little effect, save perhaps in the case of those carefully considered crimes: the organised fraud, the commercial supply of drugs, terrorism, or other carefully planned criminal activity. There is a case to be made here that such criminals should know that the stakes are high. It also has to be said that most people in our society have much better reasons to avoid crime than the fear of punishment, as students in my lectures have appreciated when I have asked them why they do not go out to rob old people in order to supplement their student means!

The second reason for higher levels of sentence is not only a public refusal to accept that anything other than prison is not really a punishment at all, but also an increasing inability in offenders themselves to manage a non-custodial sentence. From the reports we read on offenders, so many have intellectual impairment, family disadvantage, and lack of social skills that rehabilitation, with its demands for change, is innately difficult; quite apart from a prevailing general indifference to consequence or concern for the future.

Thirdly, there is the advent of sentencing guidelines. In principle these make sense, as in the past there has been much justified disquiet over inconsistencies in sentencing around the country and between courts. However, they do seem (whether intentionally or not) to have ratcheted up sentencing. There was great public criticism when it was thought that a new guideline reduced the 'tariff' for domestic burglary or drugs, but there will be no criticism if the move is the other way. Starting points are higher than perhaps they used to (or need to) be.

The last reason is more philosophical. Classic penal theory concentrated on the culpability of the offender, and that was what the sentence essentially reflected. Now, there is a much greater focus on the consequence of the criminal activity rather than just on what the offender intended. This can best be seen in three types of case.

The first relates to death caused by driving. There may be many levels of culpability involved ranging from momentary inattention at a traffic light, through to a reckless disregard for other road users or road traffic laws. The consequence for the victim, however, will always be the same and will usually be devastating to their family. It is not normally difficult to explain the heavy sentence on the reckless driver with previous motoring convictions who drove at 70 miles an hour in a 30 mile an hour limit and killed a baby in a pram being pushed over a zebra crossing with a car already stationary there. It is, however, much harder to explain the significantly lighter sentence on the tired driver, who was otherwise a good citizen, but who misjudged and jumped the amber light – to take two examples from my court.

A second type of case is that involving very serious injuries to young children, often by shaking. The culpability may be the momentary loss of control under considerable stress. The consequence may be a lifelong disability in the child. It is very difficult to find a sentence that justly reflects culpability without belittling the consequence.

Again, with two young men, usually while having been drinking, who square up to fight but one, either because of an unknown condition or a freakish fall, dies. The disparity between culpability and consequence is again obvious. The increasing reflection of the consequence in the sentence inevitably involves a significant increase in the tariff. While, of course, no judge can disregard the consequence of a crime, I have to say that I am uneasy at the modern trend. For me, the principal purpose of the sentence is to punish the offender, and that therefore his culpability should be the dominant consideration. The statute[1] requires that the sentence is to be commensurate with the seriousness of the offence and that is not quite the same thing.

However all this may be, and however important it may be, we are concerned in this book with reflecting on the discretionary powers of the judge. In an age of sentencing guidelines, with a new weight given to consequence and increasing statutory controls over sentence, how much room does a judge have to exercise discretion in an individual case? Is sentencing becoming less an art (as we have always believed it to be) and more a science?

To answer that we must go first to another essentially philosophical question: what is the purpose of a sentence? Many answers can be (and are) given to that question. Deterrence: you have been beastly and we will now be especially beastly to you so

---

[1]   Section 80(2), Powers of Criminal Courts (Sentencing) Act 2000.

that you and others will be deterred. Retribution: you have been beastly so we shall be beastly to you in just proportion. Reformation: you have been beastly but we are not going to be beastly to you in the hope that you will see there are better things in life than being beastly. You can add to all that expiation, compensation and, of course, the current statutory requirement we have noted, that the sentence is commensurate.[2] Now, each of those are I think morally justifiable approaches. However, it is obvious that they usually will pull in different directions. The choice of purpose will have a significant impact on the actual sentence passed, and that choice still belongs to the judge.

Then you feed in two further matters. First, guidelines are just that. They are not a grid from which the judge simply reads off the appropriate sentence, as is said to happen in some states of the USA. A judge may depart from guidelines – up or down – provided reasons for so doing are given. Secondly, the bases on which the Court of Appeal can interfere with the sentence are threefold: wrong in principle, manifestly excessive, or unduly lenient.[3] Those matters together demonstrate that, in addition to the choice of purpose, a considerable discretion is still left to the individual judge. The requirement, as in other areas of discretion, is to explain your reasons for your decision.

What all this means in practice is this: the judge must start with the guidelines and that will provide the starting point. The judge must then deal with any aggravating or mitigating feature identified in the guidelines or specific to the case and then adjust the starting point up or down accordingly. That will produce the sentence actually passed in many cases. However, the judge has a discretion to act differently – perhaps this is a case where deterrence is really justified, or perhaps a case where there is a

---

[2] See also purposes of sentencing: ss 142 and 142A, Criminal Justice Act 2003.

[3] See, eg, *R v Waddington* (1983) Cr AppR (S) 66, and see also Criminal Justice Act 1988, ss 35, 36 for prosecution appeals.

real prospect of reformation. A choice of either approach will significantly affect the final sentence, perhaps radically, and, I believe, rightly so.

The judiciary has always upheld what has come to be known as the prerogative of mercy, however little they may in fact employ it. It finds fine expression in Portia's speech in the *Merchant of Venice*:

> 'The quality of mercy is not strained;
> It droppeth as the gentle rain from heaven
> Upon the place beneath. It is twice blessed;
> It blesses him that gives and him that takes:
> ...
> It is an attribute to God himself;
> And earthly power doththen show likest God's
> When mercy seasons justice.'[4]

It finds more prosaic expression in the words, 'There but for the grace of God go I!'

Now one has to recognise that mercy involves a mitigation of justice, the conscious passing of a sentence that is less than commensurate and less than that deserved. It is, in modern penal policy, necessarily controversial. It is, however, a principle that the judiciary is keen to uphold, in theory at least. When might a judge exercise the discretion to show mercy? For me, it can arise in four types of case.

First, where there is something deeply unusual about the case itself. I remember defending an elderly man charged with murder as a result of discovering that his wife was much older than she had ever said she was and he had, in his distress, strangled her with his tie. He then tried to gas himself, but he had not put enough money in the meter and so had failed. It was a case for mercy, and mercy he received.

---

4   Act IV, scene 1.

The second type of case is where there is some truly exceptional personal element. Thus, I have exercised mercy where an offender has been diagnosed with a terminal illness or where he is the carer of someone who has been so diagnosed.

The third type of case is more controversial, and it is where the plea for mercy comes not from the offender but from the victim. You meet it in a death caused by driving case where, not unusually, driver and victim were friends and were in the same vehicle. It is argued that one family has already been damaged and another should not be also by the passing of a long sentence. These cases are particularly difficult because they produce widely differing reactions amongst victims, from open forgiveness to vengeful hate. It is difficult to justify a vastly different sentence on the same facts depending only on the victim's reaction. At the same time, it would be wholly inhumane entirely to ignore such a plea for mercy. Of course, even greater scrutiny is required where the victim, for example in a domestic violence case, may still be under the influence of the offender.

The fourth occasion is perhaps the most common: where the judge is convinced that the offender is now motivated to change his life; a case where the judge is considering reformation as the key principle of the sentence. This is not always an easy call to make, as most advocates will take the 'crossroads of life' argument if remotely plausible. On the other hand, most offenders do grow out of crime in the end and usually it is brought about by a partner, a family, or a proper job – these, and not fear of prison, are the most effective antidotes to criminal behaviour. Society stands to benefit from a proper use of mercy in such a case but has little time for the judge who calls it wrong. Yet, in my view, judges should not be cowed by the risk of failure, as a reformed and responsible citizen is a prize not to be lightly spurned. All too often, of course, judges never find out whether they were right or not.

Sometimes discretion in sentencing is severely tested by the case itself. The most obvious modern example is in sentencing an elderly man for crimes of a sexual nature committed 20, 30, or even 40 years before. A policy decision has been taken to limit (but not remove) discretion. Generally only a small discount is made for age, even though in many ways the person being sentenced is quite different to the original offender. Of course, this works the other way round too. I had to sentence a middle-aged man who had already been to prison for sexual offences. He had pleaded guilty to offences committed many years before in an institution when he was aged 16. My view was that, on the same approach, he had to be sentenced as though he were a 16-year-old of good character; his intermediate convictions being treated as irrelevant.

Another example is where the offender is unusually young. I had referred to me for sentence a 13-year-old who had pleaded guilty to the rape of his 10-year-old sister. She, of course, could not consent because of her age. He was prosecuted because they had been caught in the act by their foster mother, who had naturally informed the local authority. I asked for and obtained the care file that showed that incest had been endemic in the family for at least three generations. The boy was, of course, a serious risk to others, but his culpability was very low. A therapeutic, not a punitive, sentence was needed and, happily, good social work had indeed produced a residential unit. Inevitably there are very young offenders who must be locked up because they are a danger to society and often to themselves, but with very young offenders not only is culpability often more restricted, the prospects for reform are also much brighter.

I trust that that brief survey will at least show that, even in these days of statutory requirements and sentencing guidelines, a considerable discretion in sentencing in the individual case remains with the judge. Although circumscribed by statute and science, it seems to me that sentencing remains an art and I doubt that I am alone in having found that it was often the most difficult task of the Crown Court judge.

There are, as I have tried to show, all manner of questions of principle and practice that frequently tend in opposing directions. Quite often difficult matters of judgment arise requiring choices to be made that translate into decisions that are bound to upset someone. Of course, no judge will always read the case correctly; as I have often pointed out in this book, we are all prone to the frailties of the human condition and no one tends to be more conscious of this than the judge. On the other hand discretion enables the judge to do what seems fair, just and right in the individual case.

While the discretion committed to the Crown Court judge is both narrower and more restricted than that of the family court judge, it is the same animal. It involves making choices where more than one course of action is lawfully available. Its use may produce controversial and long-lasting consequences. It therefore comes with all the same questions. Do we as a society know the extent of these powers? Are we content that they exist in this form? Do the judges, in the exercise of these powers, act with and deserve the consent of society?

That concludes our review of discretionary power. I want now both to reflect on the broader picture and our key questions, and also to see where the future may lead and how the role of the judge may be affected.

Chapter 8

What of the Future?

The role of the modern judge has developed in response to the demands of an increasingly complex society. There is no one cause for this complexity, but it must include the range of international cultures that have had to blend with or at least co-exist alongside the host culture. This has ethnic, religious, philosophical, and lifestyle components. It must include all the new ways in which families are formed, whether by adoption, IVF, or the creation of stepfamilies, as well as new forms of family, whether with single or same-sex parents or in the context of kinship care. It must also include the increasing needs of families led by those who themselves have had no adequate experience of being parented or who suffer from mental ill-health, as well as those who prejudice their own capacity to parent by abuse of alcohol or drugs. It is not that all of this is new, but its volume and its interrelationship create a degree of complexity that is new.

The judge has found himself in a new role. Welfare and best interests tests continue to regulate family and mental capacity law, tests that depend on the individual evaluation of each particular case. That involves the judge having to have a much more profound understanding of what is happening in the society in which he serves. It also involves judges in having to balance competing religious, cultural and personal demands let alone the expectations of individual litigants. Again, as the state assumes a greater role in these areas, so the role of the judge assumes an ever greater significance in holding the ring between the State and the citizen. The power to order what is in effect a compulsory adoption and the power to direct the removal of the elderly dementia sufferer from family home to care home are two of the more striking issues that regularly confront the modern judge.

Again, as medical technology develops and more and more can be done not only to preserve and extend life but also to manipulate natural processes to desired ends, there is brought into question our ethical abilities to control and regulate these things. Few will want to argue that just because we can do it we should do it, but likewise few can agree not just on how we regulate but how we achieve a principled basis for so doing. I remember watching a television discussion on the protection of stored embryos. A distinguished panel of doctors, scientists, theologians, and philosophers could all agree that these were serious matters involving serious moral issues, and that regulation was essential. What they could not agree was the principles upon which such regulation should be founded. The Royal College of Paediatricians' guidance on the withdrawal or withholding of treatment contains much that is helpful and useful, but it is not easy to discern the basic principles in which the guidance is grounded. Perhaps the authors could not agree amongst themselves.

This has resulted in judges being drawn into value judgments, which has traditionally not been their role. The essential judgment between a child remaining in the natural family or going to an adoptive family or the tension between autonomy and protection in the best interests judgment on behalf of one who lacks capacity, involves complex value judgments which, whilst they are presented as 'welfare' or 'best interests' evaluations, are in fact a nuanced, complex, and profound distillation and balancing of values where, as we have seen, no one answer may emerge as the only reasonable outcome.

It is made more difficult because each of us has a mindset – a set of unspoken assumptions about the world and our place in it – that it rarely occurs to us to question. It comes into sharp focus when mindsets collide, for example between western liberal enlightenment and a conservative, essentially rural, Islam. I take that not because it is unique, but because it is recognisable and a common experience in family and mental capacity cases. This means that we have a difficult (it may turn out to be an impossible) task to identify and agree the basic principles on which we are to run our society in the future. Indeed, the very concepts of 'society' and 'state' may be in issue.

This is made yet more difficult by the increasing internationalisation of our world. This comprises not only the development, success, and increasing dominance of the multinational corporation, but also the increasing movement of people across the world and the availability of almost instantaneous communication everywhere. Actually it is not internationalisation that makes the difficulty, so much as the fact that most effective means of regulation, public financial control, and enforcement are constrained by national boundaries. We have seen its impact in family law, but it can be seen in almost every area of public life. Much can be done by treaty but not much by any other means, since most international conventions and bodies exist only by permission of their member states.

An interesting example may be found in European family law. Because of freedom of movement, it became necessary to deal with the question of which country's court should exercise jurisdiction in a family case. A regulation known as Brussels II was agreed and implemented in the EU (including, of course, the UK) and has become established in our law. What effect will Brexit have on this, and what will be the implications? We can only wait and see.

Although it may appear that I am straying far outside the limits of my own expertise, I think it is necessary to have as wide perspective as possible on the specific issue of the role of the judge in our society and in particular how and why discretionary powers committed to him are exercised. I have no reason to believe that our society will become any less complex or any less diverse in the foreseeable future. I also think it highly likely that, in the areas of family law and mental incapacity, judges will continue to be expected to make discretionary judgments constrained only by the statutory checklists and the facts of individual cases. It will be necessary to take account of shifts in public attitude that are just as likely to take a conservative turn as they are to pursue a liberal course; the swinging pendulum is an historical phenomenon. Those are serious challenges for judges even when operating, as they do, in a collegial setting and subject to the authority of the appellate courts and of course of Parliament.

The pursuit of truth will remain a prominent concern. All the publicity surrounding every enquiry centres on the determination of the truth; and rightly so. Nevertheless, the means by which that is attempted continue to be fallible. There are no windows into the human mind and conscience. What is important is that we do not abandon our determination to unearth truth, but that we do appreciate the human limitations on that task.

But what about some of the specific issues that will confront the judge? Some of these are particular to the legal process, like questions of access to justice and legal representation or questions as to how children and incapacitated adults can take a full part in decisions being made about them. Some are more general, like the issue of human rights as against the sovereignty of Parliament or the handling of apparent conflicts of public opinion like the protection of family privacy as against the State's responsibility to protect or the conflict between autonomy and protection in determining the best interests of those who lack mental capacity. I will start with some matters particular to the legal process.

Recent changes in legal aid have greatly increased the number of parties representing themselves in the family courts. Effectively, legal aid is no longer available in private family disputes and, where it is available, in the family courts and in the Court of Protection, it is subject to a merits test (is there a properly arguable case?) and an increasingly stringent means test. The exception to that is where the State seeks to intervene in private family life, for example in taking care proceedings, when parents do qualify for legal aid without a means or merits test. Judges, especially the District Judges, are building up experience and expertise in dealing with cases where parties are representing themselves.

There are two sets of circumstances which each requires a different approach. One is where some parties are represented by lawyers and some are not, and the other is where all parties are unrepresented. In the latter case most formal rules of procedure have to be drastically modified or even put aside. Eyeball to eyeball confrontation in cross-examination in these cases has, in my experience, never achieved anything of use to the judge, but is often emotionally damaging, particularly where, as parents, they are going to have to deal with each other over their children for perhaps many years to come. If the dispute between the parents is simply a decision over some specific issue or over living arrangements, where both parents accept that the other has a significant continuing role to play in the lives of their children, a relaxation of rules even to the point where the hearing becomes a three-way discussion (or four ways if a Cafcass officer is present) can be productive. Where, however, there is a serious dispute of fact or welfare dispute so profound that neither parent can be relied on to put their children's interests first, it can be much more difficult.

Sometimes that can be resolved by making the children parties with separate representation (but only occasionally possible because of the human and financial resource implications), or a judge must devise means to secure in that particular case a fair and full hearing.

The second set of circumstances I found more difficult: where some adult parties were represented and some not. The legally represented party has to be allowed to put their case and the unrepresented party must be able to put their case too; an individual blend of formality and informality is needed. Advocates can usually be relied upon to deal fairly and openly with the unrepresented parties, but in the end they do have a specific client. The emphasis has to be upon fairness; if that is preserved, then the judge has a considerable degree of latitude over procedure. That demands some degree of judicial imagination. I have found, for example, that it is helpful to allow the unrepresented party to set out their case first, for what they most want is that the judge should hear and understand their case. That often leads both to a reduction in tension and the avoidance of unhelpful cross-examination.

In approaching litigants in person, the judge has to hold the ring between ensuring that the parties' best case is before the court and preventing abuse of the court process by the vindictive, the manipulative, the bully, or the obsessive; all characters sadly familiar to the family judge. With greater numbers representing themselves, these questions will assume larger prominence in the future. There will always be disappointed litigants aggrieved at the result whereas the contented tend to remain silent. It will not be possible to please all or to avoid criticism, which may be loud and strident, let alone to avoid error for all the reasons that we have seen. This remains a human exercise involving fallible human parties and a human judge where there may be more than one reasonable view and one reasonable outcome. Of course not everyone will be happy, but a decision is nevertheless required.

There has rightly been strong pressure over the last few years to enable those, whether children or incapacitated adults, to take a greater part in the making of decisions which will affect their lives, perhaps with lifelong consequences. That includes seeing the child. However, we do have to recognise the inherent artificiality of that process. First, it is necessary to be clear what the purpose of such a meeting is: is it to give evidence, or express views, or simply to meet the person who is the decision-maker? That sets the framework for the meeting. Secondly, no child can have a truly private conversation with the judge. Not only must someone else be present and the meeting recorded, but also the child cannot be promised confidentiality as matters may arise where fairness (or safeguarding) demands that a parent has the chance to answer. That is not a normal basis for a child to meet a stranger.

All that said, no child who wants such a meeting should usually be denied it; likewise, no child should be compelled to one. The usefulness of such meetings will have to be judged from the experience of them. My own experience is essentially positive, although I have met a wall of silence. What is essential is that every child should feel that they have had the opportunity they want to influence the outcome. The same should apply to any adult about whom decisions are to be made. They cannot dictate the outcome, but they should certainly have an opportunity to influence it.

The question of children having control over their own bodies will remain controversial. It is right that we afford young adults autonomy, but it is right, too, that we do not sacrifice our responsibility as adults on the altar of autonomy. No child should bear responsibility for bringing about their own death, and thus some restriction on autonomy is likely to remain. It is frankly difficult to see Parliament deciding otherwise, much less that judges should take the law in that direction.

Yet many will continue to go unheard, for example children who
are too young or adults who are too disabled, and those whose
views cannot be disentangled from the views of those who care
for them. It is, however, important to remember that simple
wishes can be ascertained in very young children as well as in
seriously learning disabled adults. There are two other large
groups who go unheard: children whose parents have reached
agreement amongst themselves, and adults whose families have
agreed arrangements with the local authority or a hospital. In
the second case hopefully the adult's views will have been
sought, but no proceedings or investigation may be necessary if
compliance with an agreement can be obtained. In the case of
children this is the usual position, as most parents do agree.
Some research into children in this position conducted some
time ago through Liverpool University revealed considerable
dissatisfaction especially amongst older children. Given,
however, pressure on courts and resources, and the general trend
of supporting parental agreements, it is difficult to see a way
through this other than to impress on parents the need to keep
their children properly informed and involved. To require every
separating family to submit their arrangements to State scrutiny
would not only be very expensive, but may well be seen as an
unwarranted intrusion into family life. This may simply be one
of many examples where a judge has to accept that children
cannot be spared all the consequences of what those who care
for them choose to do or not do. It may also illustrate that in the
real world concepts of welfare are often constrained by simple
practicalities.

Confidentiality can present real difficulties in family proceedings. Children cannot be promised confidentiality, as we have
seen, and the same will generally apply with the adult who lacks
capacity. This can present real problems where the child or adult
is bursting to tell you something but she does not want a parent
or family member to know that she has said it. It gets even more
complicated when – and I have had this – the police turn up at

the family hearing saying they have information which they will only reveal to judge, for example that the father has taken out a contract on the mother's life, the mother knows nothing of it, and the father does not know that he is being investigated. The judge is in an impossible position: one can neither ignore, nor (save in the very short-term) withhold it. How to deal with these problems without allowing the development of complex trials within already complex trials is still a work in progress. After all, the information may be true, or it may be malicious, or it may simply be the mistaken product of Chinese Whispers.

Confidentiality within the trial is often also in tension with the publicity of the trial. Whether the issue is who may attend or what may be reported or what may be broadcast, the concern is to maintain fairness to both the public and the parties whilst giving the judge the greatest opportunity of deciding a case on all the relevant evidence. In the end, Parliament may have to make a judgment as to the balance between confidentiality and fairness but, unless and until it does, the trial judge will be left with the responsibility of striking that balance in each individual case.

As well as these more specific matters, there are some general issues that are going to impinge on our thinking as a society. We have seen them in passing but their prominence is likely to increase.

We have already thought in some detail about the tension between autonomy and protection in the making of adult best interest decisions. I think the primary focus is likely to be on older people who suffer from a degree of dementia. In particular, it will arise in the context of care at home or in a care home. These disputes can generate enormous emotional force and examples are readily found in the media. At present, cases are dealt with on a case-by-case basis as a best interests judgment made by a judge, or it is at least open to scrutiny by the court. Whether that will continue or whether another way can be found will be a matter of public debate.

It is difficult to foresee any change from the present inclination in practice to favour protection over autonomy, especially when urgent decisions are required. It is true that there are some strong advocates of autonomy but, in the aftermath of events like the Rotherham sex abuse scandal, that approach is likely to be favoured more in theory than in practice. Likewise, I see little prospect of an increased precedence being given to emotional, rather than physical, welfare. It is very difficult to criticise public officials for not taking decisions that are likely, however well-intentioned they may be, to expose them to public criticism which can be merciless. If as a society we cannot learn to accept that honest mistakes will be made in an attempt to do the best for someone, then this defensiveness is bound to persist.

There remains the tension between guarding the integrity and privacy of the family on the one hand, and giving effect to a generally acknowledged duty in the State to protect its children and vulnerable adults on the other. What is perceived by one as a threat to the integrity of the family is seen by another as the fulfilment of the State's duty to protect. It arises every time the protection involves a removal from the family. Once again these questions generate enormous emotional force, and once again examples are readily found in the media. If it can be said that the media are a little too ready to respond to individual complaints against the state, and that the agents of the state are a little too defensive in their response, it does not hide the fact that there are real issues and that there is all too often more than one reasonable view and more than one reasonable outcome available. The way judges operate at present is to make removal from the family the option of last resort, but quite often initial decisions have to be made under pressure of time and with incomplete information. That sometimes results in an initial authorisation of a removal that then has to be re-considered in the light of much more information and investigation. It is, of course, very unwise to take risks with safety on the basis of partial information.

It must be the case that adoption, or at least our current concept of it, will remain controversial. It sits uneasily with traditional concepts of family responsibility and integrity and with liberal concepts of the rights of parents. It does, however, offer huge benefits to children who would otherwise face an unending cycle of deprivation and abuse that they in turn would be likely to impose on their children. Of course we must beware social engineering, but not at the price of tolerating significant harm. Adoption generates strong views on all sides, and the adoption process is both emotive and dramatically final. Future controversy is inevitable, but it is difficult not to see adoption playing a significant role in child protection in the future.

All this raises the question as to the nature and extent of the discretion that is conferred on judges by our society. We have noted both the warning words of Lord Bingham and the fact that they do not always sit easily with family or mental capacity law. Of course discretion is not entirely unfettered, but it is very wide-ranging, directed by (but not confined to) the statutory checklists and with no guidance as to what weight to attach to any particular aspect of any individual case. Perhaps when we could speak meaningfully of agreed social norms and values this did not matter so much, but in today's society it confers very great power on the individual judge. As we have seen, moreover, provided he has taken into account everything that is relevant and reached a decision reasonably open on the evidence, the appellate courts are deeply reluctant to interfere. To that extent his power is even greater.

The alternative, as we have noted, is a more rule-based approach that may give rise to greater certainty of outcome but also to greater risk of injustice in a particular case. That pressure has been increasingly present in sentencing since being subject to guidelines. However, enough discretion remains to prevent individual injustice. Rules may, of course, operate more readily where there are agreed norms and values. Where that is no longer the case, one must wonder quite what sort of meaningful rule could be devised even to give a starting point beyond those matters in the statutes which judges are already bound to take into account. Any rule would rapidly acquire so many exceptions, qualifications, and glosses as to deprive it of all utility. Whatever the drawbacks (and they are real enough) of discretionary welfare decisions, they do at least allow full value to be given to the particular needs of each child or vulnerable adult whose future is in question.

However, even in areas not directly involved in human relationships, rule enforcement can be difficult. There remains a continuing debate about the distribution of property on divorce. While property is arguably more susceptible to control by rule than questions of welfare or best interests, it is not free from difficulty. Parliament has thus far shown no appetite for a major revision of the property provisions in the Matrimonial Causes Act 1973.

We also noted the tensions that can arise between welfare and social policy and we looked at the court's experiences in dealing with international commercial surrogacy arrangements. There is simply no general agreement about surrogacy either in the world, or in Europe, or probably in the UK. The debate on our domestic laws will continue. The problem arises where people go abroad to do what is lawful there but is not here: something that may become increasingly common. There is a choice to be made between simple enforcement of the domestic law, irrespective of consequence, and a course that recognises the position of the person (usually a child) who had no say in the matter. It is clear that many countries, both Western and Eastern, are now confronting this question and there is as yet no generally agreed approach. No doubt these issues will arise in other contexts as medical science advances. What can be said, I think, with some confidence is that, if the decision is left with the judge, the innocent and powerless will not be made to pay the price of the decision of others. That view at least seems to resonate with judges of many jurisdictions.

A further area of potential difficulty is the relationship between the judiciary and Parliament, particularly in the context of the Human Rights Act. The United Kingdom is unusual, if not unique, both in having no written constitution and also in its concept of the sovereignty of Parliament which, while it may be restricted by voluntarily accepted conventions, has theoretically no limit on its powers; quite unlike the usual position where there is a written constitution and a court with jurisdiction to interpret and enforce it. As with many British institutions, its essential justification lies in the fact that it has worked. The Human Rights Act 1998 has put a gloss on this. Whilst the court cannot strike down an Act, it can declare an Act, or an individual provision within it, to be inconsistent with the Convention and this requires Parliament to reconsider it. Although Parliament cannot be compelled by the court to change the legislation, there is an accelerated procedure in the Act to allow Parliament to do so. Moreover, the court is to interpret any Act, wherever it is possible to do so, in compliance with the Convention. This is not the place for a detailed critique of these matters but, in the context of our discussion, it provides a further illustration of how judges are drawn into policy questions much more than has traditionally been the case and how they have been charged with the particularly delicate task of balancing and resolving conflicts of rights. The whole issue is firmly on the political agenda and likely to remain so for the foreseeable future.

How it will be resolved, I cannot say. Ironically, if we do move to a Bill of Rights or even to a written constitution, the consequence is likely to be investing yet more, if rather different, powers in judges as a Bill of Rights or a written constitution will be susceptible to judicial interpretation. However, it seems likely that, whatever is done, the implementation and enforcement of those rights and individual cases will continue to fall to judges, and will come with a considerable discretionary element as rights and conflicts of rights are worked out in individual cases.

What is important, however, is that the principle is decided where possible in Parliament: assisted dying is a case in point. It feels uncomfortable that possible conviction for assisting a suicide is a matter for prosecutorial discretion, just as the withdrawal of artificial nutrition or hydration is a matter of judicial discretion. Of course these issues are very difficult to manage through Parliament, let alone to get them decided. Sometimes there must be a temptation to leave issues to judicial discretion rather than to decide principle by statute. However, surely these matters in the end should be decided by the elected chamber with the assistance of the House of Lords rather than left to be teased out on a case-by-case basis by the judiciary? However much that approach may accord with traditional patterns of thought, the difficulty with doing things on this basis is that you may end up incrementally at a place you would never have wanted to go to when you first set out. Clear principles can to a great extent overcome that risk.

The more I reflect on this question of judicial discretion (and I have thought on it much, particularly over the last 12 years or so), the more I find myself mindful of the power that the exercise of a wide discretion vests in the judge, not least in relation to those involved in the particular case. We have the power because Parliament directly and indirectly has committed it to us. Some powers in the inherent jurisdiction of the High Court are derived from the prerogative powers of the sovereign as *parens patriae*, the father of the people, but Parliament has chosen generally to allow the judiciary to retain and develop those powers. It has intervened only occasionally, as it did with the curtailing of the powers of Wardship in the Children Act 1989 by preventing judges placing children in care on welfare grounds alone, making the route to care exclusively that provided by the Act.

We must now return finally to the basic questions that have underpinned this book: what is the true ethical and legal basis of these powers, and are they exercised with the informed consent of the society in whose name we act? These two questions are interrelated and, I suggest, of fundamental importance in a democratic society.

I have tried to address these questions through frank reflections on my own judicial experience and on the fallibility of the process and the people involved. I chose the route of child welfare and best interests of those who lack capacity to make their own decisions, as well as that of criminal sentencing, because they reflect that experience and also because they are the most controversial manifestations of the discretionary powers of the modern judge.

These powers have their roots in statute but, as I hope I have shown, they allow a considerable breadth in decision-making. The purpose is to allow the judge to do justice in the individual case – that is the ethical principle upon which discretion is founded. That comes at a price: not only in some lack of certainty of outcome, but some lack of certainty in the values inherent in the decision-making process itself, as the judge seeks to balance the values of society, the values of those involved in the case and his own personal value system – and this is as true in sentencing as in anything else. It often involves resolving the tension between good but, frequently in the individual case, irreconcilable, principles. The tensions between transparency and privacy in the administration of justice, between protection and autonomy in best interests decisions or between punishment and reform in criminal sentencing are but examples of that. In the end, choices have to be made.

It is therefore important to ask whether these powers are indeed exercised, and choices made, with the informed consent of the society in whose name we act. I am troubled about that, not least because I am unconvinced that the full range of these powers and the choices that have to be made are indeed widely understood today. One of my aspirations in this book has been to describe those powers and choices in a manner that is reasonably accessible to any interested person. Otherwise, any consent may not be truly informed consent.

At the heart of this issue lies the question of trust. An informed public nevertheless has to trust judges to exercise these powers in a way to which the public may give their consent. In a democracy based on the separation of powers, judges must be independent not only of executive control, but of overbearing pressure from media, pressure groups, and general noise in the public square. That is not in any way to suggest that judicial decisions should not be open to legitimate criticism. We must be aware of and take account of such matters, but we must also retain independence. Independence requires trust, and trust requires that choices and values should be politically and ethically acceptable.

I think as judges we are very aware of that element of trust and the need to ensure not only that it is maintained, but that it is deserved and rightly placed in us. A small illustration of that, to my mind, is found in the way that people generally behave in court. With vast personal issues at stake, disorder, rudeness and ill-temper are sufficiently rare that they tend to stick in the memory. Most, however awful the outcome for them, bear themselves with courage and dignity. That speaks to me not of the imposition of naked or capricious power but of an element of respect and trust that those powers will be used wisely, fairly and to the best of the judge's personal ability.

Trust is essential, but it must be deserved, too. There is a requirement on judges not only to act with integrity (and to be beyond corruption), but with a real understanding of the needs and aspirations of the society they serve. I go further. I do not think that the powers that we have been discussing can be effectively exercised without an understanding of that society and a genuine empathy with humanity, even when it goes horribly wrong. The recluse and the cynic have no place on the Bench. A humane understanding of people, a deep sympathy with human fallibility, and a desire for a just and ordered society must be indispensable features of the judiciary. It is the combination of humility in our approach to a case and confidence in deciding it that should be the hallmark of the judge. Only so can judges deserve, enjoy, and retain the trust of the society among whom we are authorised to exercise these extensive and remarkable discretionary powers.